BIG CITY FIRE TRUCKS
VOLUME I • 1900 -1950

Donald F. Wood & Wayne Sorensen

Dedication

to the memory of Ed Gardner 1925-1995

Founding president of the Sacramento Fire Buff Club; fire dispatcher; firefighter;
fire apparatus and supply salesman; and fire historian.

© 1996 by

Donald F. Wood and Wayne Sorensen

Published by

**krause
publications**

700 E. State Street • Iola, WI 54990-0001
Telephone: 715/445-2214

Please call or write for our free catalog of automotive publications. Our toll-free number to
place an order or obtain a free catalog is 800-258-0929 or please use our regular business
telephone 715-445-2214 for editorial comment
and further information.

Library of Congress Catalog Number: 96-76690
ISBN: 0-87341-340-7
Printed in the United States of America

Contents

Preface

*I*n 1993 Krause Publications published a book of ours, *American Volunteer Fire Trucks*, which dealt with small-town fire apparatus frequently manned by volunteers. Most of the apparatus covered in that book were outfitted on commercial truck and bus chassis.

In this book, which is actually in two volumes, we look at big city apparatus, with the word *big* modifying both *city* and *apparatus,* for featured here are apparatus associated with big city, full-time professional departments that had large engines and trucks. Big cities had the aerial ladder trucks and water towers that were not found in small-town America. Most of the big city equipment was built by "name" manufacturers and considered as "custom," and would carry names such as American-LaFrance or Seagrave. These custom builders also outfitted some commercial trucks. A Dodge chassis outfitted by Seagrave would be referred to as a Dodge/Seagrave. A surprisingly large number of apparatus were built in the shops of major city fire departments, taking advantage of the paid firefighters' underutilized time.

This volume covers the period from about 1900 until 1950. The second volume will cover 1951 to the present.

We thank all the photograph sources, whom we hope are accurately covered in the credit lines. The late Martha Cedar of White Trucks was the generous source of all the photos credited Volvo/White. We appreciate the help of Ernest N. Day, of New Jersey Fire Equipment Corporation, and of Tamara Wood. Thanks also to Janet Ward of *American City & County* for permission to reproduce an old cartoon.

Several persons support a fund at San Francisco State University that supports old truck research. We acknowledge some of the donors: Stuart B. Abraham, Edward C. Couderc of Sausalito Moving & Storage, Gilbert Hall, David Kiely, ROADSHOW, Gene Olson, Oshkosh Truck Foundation, Charlie Wacker, and Bill West.

Wayne Sorensen
San Jose State University

Donald F. Wood
San Francisco State University

Introduction

$\mathcal{A}$t the beginning of the 20th Century, fire apparatus in U.S. cities were horse-drawn. Since horses could run at top speed for only about one-half mile, there were numerous fire stations. Fires were reported by using electric alarm boxes that were at most major street corners.

Motorized apparatus were introduced in about 1905, and the period from then until about 1920 witnessed the replacement of the horse. Many early motorized rigs were tractors that were placed in front of horse-drawn pumpers or ladders. An evolutionary step was using the truck's engine to both propel the vehicle and power the pump or aerial ladder.

The decade of the 1920s was probably the most explosive in terms of spreading auto culture throughout the U.S. This included widespread adoption of trucks in commercial markets, in which they had begun competing with railroads. The improvements in quality and dependability of trucks was also reflected in the fire apparatus field. Many of the fire engines and trucks built during the 1920s served in first-line assignments through World War II.

During the 1930s, motor trucks evolved to the point that they could be considered "modern." Relatively few improvements remained to be made. Hydraulics had replaced mechanics in truck brakes and in devices for raising aerial ladders.

The 1940s consisted of two distinct halves in terms of apparatus. During World War II, large numbers of 1940-style rigs were produced for military and civilian defense needs. Immediately after the war, these same styles were sold to cities that were replacing apparatus overdue for retirement from first-line service. In 1947 American-LaFrance, which had been building some cab-forward apparatus since the late 1930s, introduced its cab-forward 700 Series. This model was very popular, and within a decade or so, competitors would follow. That is a topic to be covered in Volume Two of this series.

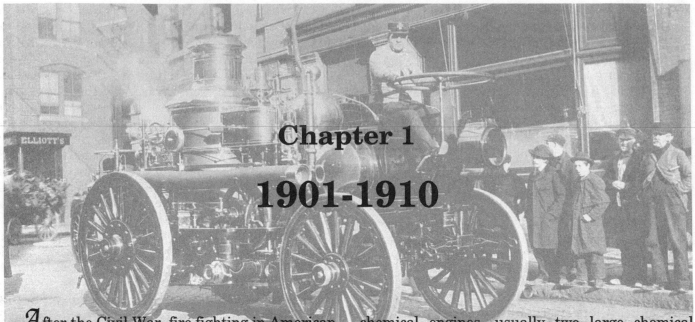

Chapter 1
1901-1910

*A*fter the Civil War, fire fighting in American cities was in the age of steam and horses, with horse-drawn, steam-powered pumpers being the backbone of municipal equipment. This type of system required paid firefighters who would tend to the horses. Within cities with paid departments, disciplined organizations were formed, promoting a spirit of professionalism.

Alarm systems were developed during this period. Before the turn of the century, most large cities had electric alarm systems tied to fire alarm boxes that were placed at most intersections and in major buildings. When the alarm was turned in, firefighters at all stations could hear it, and knew whether it was in the area to which they must respond. At the fire site, the ranking officer could call in additional alarms by sending special signals through the same alarm box. Early in the century, telephones came into use and became an even easier method of summoning the fire department.

When the alarm sounded during the horse-drawn era, stall doors would open and the horses would take their place in front of the apparatus. The driver would tug a rope, releasing harnesses that would quickly be attached to the horses. A well-trained company could leave a station in less than one minute. The driver was belted to his seat because of the rough ride and the absolute necessity that he not be thrown.

As the auto began developing at the turn of the century, all fire departments started to study the practicality of motorized apparatus. Hitching equipment was developed so that trucks and truck-tractors could be placed at the front of rigs, taking the place of horses. Equipment on the chemical engines, usually two large chemical tanks and a hose reel, was placed on regular automobile chassis, since autos could reach the fire faster than horses. Auto and truck chassis were also used to carry hose wagon and ladder bodies. A major development was the ability to use the truck's gasoline engine to propel the truck to the fire, and then to power the pump.

All motorized fire apparatus types evolved from horse-drawn and hand-drawn rigs. Pumpers are common, and are the most widely used pieces of equipment today. Hand pumpers were used up until early in this century, and horse-drawn steam pumpers were used in city departments until about World War I. (For a brief period, gasoline-powered pumps were placed on hand-drawn or horse-drawn carts.)

Pumpers require a regular and adequate water supply, and in many communities the provision of a dependable water supply was an important step in developing fire fighting capability. If there was sufficient pressure, the firefighters would run their hoses directly from the street hydrants to the fire, relying on the pumper only if they needed more pressure.

Steam pumpers were the most common large city apparatus type. Big city stations had hot water heaters that were connected to the pumper's boiler to keep the water in the boiler hot. As the engine left the station, the coupling to the heater would snap apart. The engineer would ignite wood shavings to get the boiler fire burning. It was possible to generate sufficient steam to operate the pump within three minutes. In large cities, fire departments also operated coal wagons, which carried coal in canvas bags. The steam pumper's engineer would sound the steamer's whistle to signal that they needed more coal. In some cities, the coal wagon was also equipped with a deck gun fed by hose lines from several pumpers.

In larger cities, hose wagons were used in conjunction with pumpers. Early hose carts were merely large hose reels mounted between two large wheels, and pulled by men or, later, by horses. Large wheels were necessary for use on rough pavement. Four-wheel wagons, again either hand-drawn or horse-drawn, were also used. (This practice would continue in large cities in the motorized age, with the pumper stopping at the hydrant while the hose truck carried hose from the pumper to the burning structure.) Hose wagons also carried chemical equipment and other tools. Today, hose wagons are no longer in use.

One apparatus type that has virtually disappeared is the chemical fire engine, which was hand-drawn, horse-drawn, or motorized. Chemical engines originated in France to fight small fires. At the fire site, some acid would be added, creating a pressurized foam consisting of water and CO_2. The tank would be connected to a hose that would feed it onto the fire. The chemical engine was not capable of coping with a large fire, but it could be placed into service quickly. Chemical cars consisted of one or two large, soda-acid-type extinguishers with a hose reel. At the fire site, acid in one tank would be activated and the tank's contents would discharge through the hose. The second tank would then be activated while the first one was recharged. The operator would need additional quantities of soda and acid to continue charging the tanks, as well as a supply of water. Chemical tanks were also placed on hose wagons, pumpers, and ladder trucks. The Babcock Manufacturing Company of Chicago was probably the best-known manufacturer of chemical tanks and extinguishers; Holloway was another U.S. manufacturer. In addition to separate apparatus, hand-carried extinguishers (similar to the soda-acid extinguishers used up until a few years ago) were also used by firefighters, and carried on all types of apparatus. Eventually, chemical systems were replaced by small water tanks and hoses, called booster tanks, which served about the same purpose. Credit for developing the booster tank belongs to Charles H. Fox of Ahrens-Fox fame. Today, it is known that water is as effective a fire-quelling agent as was the CO_2 produced by the soda-acid chemical tanks and extinguishers.

As cities and their structures grew, firefighters needed a way to transport ladders and hooks so they could pull down frame walls to prevent fires from spreading. Hand-drawn ladder trucks were introduced in Philadelphia in 1799. (A tiller was later added to the rear axle to help the truck turn.) Ladder trucks carried an assortment of ladders and specialized rescue tools, and were sometimes called city service trucks. There are different types of ladder trucks; for example, aerial ladders have one ladder that is raised by mechanical or hydraulic means. Snorkels (a post World War II development) have an elevated fire fighting platform, and in some situations are more maneuverable than aerial ladder trucks. Variations of aerial ladders and towers are continually being developed.

Today's rigs are still categorized by the number of different fire fighting functions they perform. A "triple combination" pumper, sometimes referred to as "pumper" in the captions used in this book, carries a pump, a large diameter 2-1/2-inch or greater hose, a larger diameter hose to connect with hydrants, a stiff suction hose to take water from streams, a booster tank and booster hose reel, ground ladders, and a variety of other fire fighting equipment such as axes, nozzles, lanterns, and crowbars.

A quad carries all the equipment mentioned in the previous paragraph, plus a complement of long ground ladders. A quint has everything a quad carries, plus an aerial ladder.

Some fire departments operate rescue squads, which consist of trucks carrying an extensive assortment of equipment needed to rescue people from fires, natural disasters, or accidents. Today, one also sees paramedic vehicles, ambulances, and hazardous spill response trucks operated by fire departments.

Salvage corps were initially operated by consortia of insurance companies to protect the property and merchandise of their specific clients from smoke and water damage. They date back several centuries. Emmons E. Douglass, in his book about salvage corps, *While the Flames Raged,* followed the histories of salvage corps in about twenty U.S. cities. Here are some of the equipment acquisitions he reported as taking place during this early decade: "In 1905, the Underwriters Salvage Corps of Cincinnati, Ohio had a salvage truck built on a Winton chassis. This was apparently the first motorized fire truck in the country."[1] Starting in 1907 the Boston Protective Department began

---

[1] Emmons E. Douglass. *While the Flames Raged* (Middletown, NY: 1993), p. 42.

motorizing by using Knox chassis. In the same year, the Chicago Fire Insurance Patrol placed a Woods Electric into service and, before the decade was over, added a Knox and some Plymouths (built by the Commercial Motor Company of Plymouth, Ohio). Also in 1907, the Underwriters Salvage Corps in St. Louis converted a Locomobile auto into a salvage unit. In Worcester, Massachusetts, the salvage corps was known as the Worcester Protective Department and its first motorized unit was mounted on a 1909 Thomas Flyer chassis.

Existing pump and ladder apparatus builders, such as American-LaFrance, Seagrave, Ahrens-Fox, and Pirsch (who will be discussed in more detail shortly) developed their own motor truck chassis. (In this book, these rigs will be referred to as "custom.") However, these custom apparatus builders had excess plant capacity and found that they could earn additional income by supplying their pumps and related equipment—which already had a reputation for quality—on lower cost, mass-produced makes of truck chassis, such as Ford, Dodge, or Chevrolet. The truck chassis (and sometimes, auto chassis) were referred to as commercial chassis and consisted of the wheels mounted on the frame, the engine and transmission, the front fenders, the hood, the cowl, and sometimes even the cab. This chassis was shipped to an apparatus outfitter who finished and equipped it into a complete piece of fire apparatus, ready to go. The distinctions between custom apparatus and those on commercial chassis will be discussed further; although, in this book we will emphasize the custom chassis used in the fire service. (In *American Volunteer Fire Trucks*, published in 1993 and available from Krause Publications, we emphasize apparatus on commercial truck chassis.)

This chapter deals with the first decade of the century when gasoline-powered autos and trucks were just coming into use. There were already a number of prominent fire apparatus builders in the U.S., and they specialized in building steam pumpers, or wagons or carts for carrying ladders, chemical tanks, or hose. During this decade, their managers must have followed with interest the auto's development and wondered when and how it would impact upon their operation. By the decade's end, a number of these "name" builders of pump and ladder apparatus would take tentative steps toward motorizing their product. Many of the firms discussed would become well-known suppliers of "custom" apparatus. For a few years early in the century, there was great interest in gasoline-powered pumps that would be hand-drawn or horse-drawn. Their advantage over steamers was that it was not necessary to maintain a continuous small fire in order to be ready to generate steam.

Ahrens-Fox was located in Cincinnati, Ohio, and its pumpers, with their highly polished globes in front, are the most distinctive of all American fire apparatus. Prior to building motorized pumpers, the firm and its predecessors were involved in building steam pumping engines. About 1890 the Ahrens Manufacturing Company of Cincinnati joined with another firm to form the American Fire Engine Company, headquartered in Seneca Falls, New York. Around 1900 this firm and others evolved into American-LaFrance. The Ahrens-Fox firm itself started in Cincinnati in 1905, spinning off from what had become American-LaFrance. Founders of the new company were Chris Ahrens, who had long ties with the family firm, and Charles Hurst Fox, assistant chief of the Cincinnati Fire Department. Fox was also responsible for designing the water tube boilers. The firm would introduce its first motorized pumper in 1911.

American-LaFrance of Elmira, New York, is the best-known of all U.S. fire apparatus manufacturers, and dates from long before the turn of the century. The initial company started in 1832 on the banks of the Erie Canal, when John F. Rogers began building "Rogers Patent Balance Fire Engine," a hand-powered pump. Late in the nineteenth century, a number of well-known manufacturers were joined in an attempt to dominate the industry, and they formed the American Fire Engine Company. This firm then became part of the International Fire Engine Company, which included most of the nation's well-known apparatus builders: LaFrance Fire Engine Company, Thomas Manning, Jr. & Co., Gleason & Bailey Mfg. Co., Chas. T. Holloway & Co., Fire Extinguisher Manufacturing Co., Macomber Fire Extinguisher Manufacturing Co., Waterous Engine Works, and Rumsey & Company.

In 1903 Asa LaFrance patented and built the first spring-powered aerial. In the same year the firm built four steam-propelled combination chemical and hose wagons. In 1904, after another reorganization, the American-LaFrance firm name was adopted. In 1905 the firm built its first motor-driven fire apparatus, a two-tank chemical on a Packard chassis, loaned to Boston. In 1909 the firm built combination chemical and hose wagons on Simplex chassis.

An early apparatus builder whose name is nearly forgotten is the Philadelphia firm of James Boyd & Brothers, dating to 1819. They initially built chemical wagons and hose wagons. Their two-wheel chemical carts came with two thirty-five-gallon copper chemical tanks, hose baskets, lanterns, a wheel-striking gong, and fifty feet of drag rope. The firm began building motorized apparatus about 1910, with an early customer being the City of Philadelphia. In 1914 Boyd built several dozen hose wagons on Mack chassis.

Front-Wheel Drive Motor Company of Hoboken, New Jersey, built what was referred to as the "Christie" tractor, which addressed the problem of supplying a tractive power unit to replace horses in front of steamers and ladders. At the end of 1910, John Walter Christie developed a two-wheel auto-tractor for the New York City Fire Department to test.

In 1898 William G. Hahn incorporated Hahn Motors in Leesport, Pennsylvania. In 1900 the firm moved to Hamburg, Pennsylvania. During this first decade, Hahn built a small number of commercial trucks.

The Howe Fire Apparatus Company started in Indianapolis in 1872, and then moved to Anderson, Indiana. They built piston-type pumps for fire department use. Howe started building horse-drawn gasoline motor pumps. In 1906 Howe built their first automotive pumper, which was sold to LaRue, Ohio. The rig could pump 250 gallons per minute in a stream 124 feet high. Its tires were made of wood, forty blocks to each wheel.

The Knox Automobile Company was founded in 1898 in Springfield, Massachusetts, and was one of the first to develop and build a water-cooled automobile. Knox's first fire apparatus was delivered to the Springfield Fire Department in 1906. It carried a "flying squad" of eight firefighters and a battalion chief who responded to all alarms. By 1909 Springfield had five Knox rigs in service, a combination chemical and hose wagon, two flying squads, and buggies for the chief engineer (as the chief was titled) and the assistant chief engineer. In 1909 the New York City's Fire Department (FDNY)'s "first piece of motorized fire apparatus was placed in service with Engine Company 72. The high pressure wagon, built by Knox, had a large hose bed and fixed turret pipe."[2] In 1909 a former Knox employee, Charles Hay Martin, returned to Springfield to become the firm's chief engineer. Martin developed a system (known as the "Martin Rocking Fifth Wheel") for attaching tractors to trailers. The turntable was carried by semi-elliptical springs attached directly to the

trailer's axle, so the weight of the trailer was carried by the tractor's rear wheels, while the much lower weight of the tractor itself was carried by lighter capacity springs. These tractors were used to take the place of horses in front of horse-drawn apparatus.

Mack, of Allentown, Pennsylvania, is a well-known truck manufacturer. At times, they marketed fire apparatus. At the turn of the century, the five Mack brothers founded this firm in Brooklyn, New York, where they built commercial buses and trucks. In 1905 they moved to Allentown, and in 1909 they built a tractor for the Allentown Fire Department to use to pull an aerial.

The Maxim Motor Company had started out in Middleboro, Massachusetts, in 1888 and built ladders for fire fighting and other uses. The firm's founder was Carlton W. Maxim, who was also an officer with the Middleboro Fire Department. He had some experience in building a motorized rig for this department.

W. S. Nott Company of Minneapolis was a well-known builder of steam pumpers at the turn of the century, with major cities such as New York, Atlanta, and Seattle as customers. In 1901 they built a gasoline-powered pumper for Gibbon, Minnesota.

Peter Pirsch & Company was a well-known fire ladder builder located in Kenosha, Wisconsin. The company was founded by Peter Pirsch, who began building apparatus in 1882. In 1899 Pirsch, son of a pioneer Wisconsin wagon builder, patented a compound trussed extension ladder. Pirsch had built early hand-drawn ladder trucks, and then horse-drawn trucks. He also was a supplier of ladders and chemical equipment to other apparatus builders. The first motorized ladder truck that Pirsch built was on a 1907 Rambler chassis. During that same year Pirsch outfitted a Jeffrey for use by the Kenosha Fire Department.

The Pope Manufacturing Company of Hartford, Connecticut, was known for building bicycles, then became involved in the manufacture of electric autos. One of its first apparatus deliveries was in 1909, a Pope-Hartford combination hose and chemical car to Bristol, Connecticut.

Robinson Fire Apparatus Manufacturing Company of St. Louis built ladders, extinguishers, nozzles, chemical engines, hook and ladder trucks, etc. In 1907 it built its first motorized apparatus, on a Chadwick automobile chassis. By 1910 the firm was assembling "custom" apparatus and

[2] John A. Calderone and Jack Lerch. *Wheels of the Bravest, a History of FDNY Fire Apparatus, 1865-1982* (Howard Beach, NY: 1984), p. 48

gave models such names as "Jumbo," "Whale," Invincible," and "Vulcan."

The Seagrave Company (now in Clintonville, Wisconsin) was founded in Detroit in 1881 by Frederick S. Seagrave, who got into the fire apparatus business indirectly. Originally, he built ladders for use in orchards. He was approached by neighboring fire departments for assistance in constructing carts for carrying ladders. Seagrave began building hand-drawn, two-wheel carts, then four-wheel ones, and soon he started building horse-drawn ladder trucks. Soon Seagrave had both feet in the fire apparatus business. In 1891 Seagrave moved his business from Detroit to Columbus, where it was to gain nationwide recognition. In 1901 Seagrave patented a spring-hoist aerial ladder. In 1907 Seagrave delivered to New York its first spring-assisted water tower. The firm was also developing its own internal combustion engines. The first customer for motorized Seagraves was Vancouver, B.C., which bought two hose wagons and a chemical wagon. In 1909 Vancouver bought several more Seagrave apparatus including a tractor-drawn aerial ladder. Seagrave soon experimented with and developed a "sidesaddle" electric-drive tractor to take the place of horses.

The Waterous Company was founded in Canada in 1844, and has been located in St. Paul, Minnesota, since 1887. It was a well-known builder of steam pumpers for many large cities. While the firm is best-known today for its pumps, for a brief period (about 1906-1918) it built complete apparatus. The first motorized pumper built in the U.S. is credited to Waterous. The date was 1906 and the rig was delivered to the Radnor Fire Company of Wayne, Pennsylvania. It had two engines, one for pumping, and one for propulsion. In 1907 Waterous delivered a motorized pumper to Alameda, California. It used a single engine for both propulsion and powering the pump. FDNY's first motorized apparatus was a Waterous.

Al C. Webb, an inventor and race car driver from Joplin, Missouri, built a chemical car on a Buick chassis for the Joplin Fire Department in 1907. In 1908 he was asked by Lansing, Michigan, to build a hose and pumping engine on an Oldsmobile chassis, which he did. Webb organized the Webb Motor Fire Apparatus Company, and located in Vincennes, Indiana. The firm prospered, reorganized, expanded, and relocated for a short time to St. Louis. In 1912 it moved to Allentown, Pennsylvania.

The White Motor Company of Cleveland started out building sewing machines and steam-powered autos. Gradually it specialized in building trucks, which it does to this day. For nearly the entire century, many apparatus outfitters have completed their bodies on White chassis. For a brief period, the firm marketed its own apparatus.

Fire apparatus were but one part of a community's fire fighting effort. A force of firefighters was also needed. Both volunteer and paid firefighters were used, with varying arrangement of compensation. Municipal water supplies were also important. The location of hydrants and the volume and pressure of water they could supply complemented the pumpers' and firefighters' capabilities. Building codes would be another fire fighting tool, as a special problem was the use of untreated wooden roof shingles, which allowed fires to spread rapidly. Properly drawn and enforced, building codes would result in safer structures.

During much of the nineteenth century, steam power was on the "cutting edge" of mechanical developments. Most large-city pumpers were powered by steam, and were horse-drawn. For a few brief years at the beginning of the twentieth century, it appeared that steam would propel many road vehicles. In the *Cycle and Automobile Trade Journal*'s second annual supplement entitled "1902 American Automobiles," twelve makes of electric autos were listed, as were forty makes with gasoline-powered internal combustion engines, and twenty-nine makes of steam-driven autos. Shown here is a rig that used steam for both propulsion and pumping. It is an 1897 Amoskeag, two cylinder 1350 gpm piston pump with a crane neck. The 17,000 pound rig was operated in Boston. It carried only suction hose and was accompanied by hose wagons. The Amoskeag Division of the Manchester Locomotive Works in Manchester, New Hampshire, started building these self-propelled pumpers in 1867. (Photo courtesy Boston Fire Department)

The fireboat *George B. McClelland*, built in 1904 for New York's fire department (FDNY), was capable of pumping 7000 gpm through sixteen discharge gates. (Photo courtesy John J. Robrecht and Dick Adelman)

A circa-1906 horse-drawn gasoline pumper built by Howe. The handles are for hand operation in case the motor failed. The rig was used in Jonesport, Maine. (Photo courtesy Dick Adelman)

LaRue, Ohio bought this pumper in about 1906. Handles at rear are for manual operation of the pump in case the truck's engine failed. A hosebox was at the rear. It was built by Howe and is one of the earliest gasoline fire engine and hosewagons built in the U.S. It was powered by a four-cylinder 32-34 hp Rutenber engine. A double clutch allowed the engine to power the pump while the truck was not moving. The tires consisted of many wooden blocks cut with the grain running toward the center of the wheel. (Photo courtesy Paul Darrell Collection)

A 1906 Packard chassis was used by American-LaFrance to outfit a chemical car that was loaned as a demonstrator to Boston. While in Boston it collided with an overhead rail track support column and was returned to the American-LaFrance plant in Elmira. After rebuilding, it was sold to Summit, New Jersey, where it served as Chemical No. 1. Equipment included two thirty-five-gallon Holloway tanks, and two Babcock hand extinguishers.

A Pope-Waverly electric chassis was outfitted by Howe for sale to Hopedale, Massachusetts, in 1906.

This is generally believed to be the first motorized pumping fire apparatus in the U.S., relying on one gasoline engine to propel the rig, and another to power a 300 gpm pump. It was built by Waterous, and delivered in 1906 to the Radnor Fire Company in Wayne, Pennsylvania. Gong in front was foot-powered. (Photo courtesy Waterous)

A Webb chemical tank on a 1907 Buick chassis. The tank held sixty gallons, and the reel held two hundred feet of hose. The rig saw service in Joplin, Missouri. (Photo courtesy Webb)

In 1907 Webb delivered this combination pump and hose car to Joplin, Missouri. It is mounted on a Packard chassis. This is possibly the first automobile combination pump and hose carrier. (Photo courtesy Webb)

Joplin, Missouri, displayed its motorized equipment in 1907. At far right is a Buick chemical car, at left front, a Packard pumper with suction hose draped over hood, and in the rear are two Thomas Flyer hose wagons. (Photo courtesy Webb)

The Boston Water Department ran this steam-powered 1907 White emergency wagon. (Photo courtesy Volvo/White)

This is a 1907 Winton operated by the Underwriters Salvage Corps in Cincinnati. Insurance companies operated these patrols to protect the contents of clients' buildings from smoke and water damage. (Photo courtesy Wayne Sorensen Collection)

Knox was a favorite make of truck purchased by fire departments prior to World War I. This is a 1908 model serving as a combination hose and squad car in Springfield, Massachusetts. Mounted on the roof is the Pompier ladder for scaling the side of buildings. An acetylene gas tank powers the headlights and the floodlight. The body, built locally, is called a "Springfield" style and has firemen sitting inside. Note also tire chains on all wheels. The firefighters' collective grimace is caused by the length of time the photographer needed to expose the film in order to take the picture. (Photo courtesy Wayne Sorensen Collection)

In large cities, fire chiefs were often titled "chief engineer." This chief engineer's "buggy" was used in Washington, D.C. It was a 1908 Carter two-engine car capable of being operated by either or both engines. Carter cars were built in Hyattsville, Maryland, and the two-engine design was a "fail-safe" provision in case one engine failed. The idea did not catch on and production lasted only two years, 1907 and 1908. (Photo courtesy Wayne Sorensen Collection)

Lansing, Michigan, where Oldsmobiles are built, bought this 1908 Oldsmobile/Webb pump and hose car. (Photo courtesy Webb)

This 1909 Seagrave Type AC-90 aerial ladder was sold to Vancouver, B.C. The seventy-five-foot aerial is shown holding six firemen. The ladder was made of wood and raised by compressed spring action. The tractor was a Seagrave AC-90, meaning that it was air-cooled and rated at 90 horsepower. It had four cylinders. By the fall of 1917, Vancouver had become Canada's first completely motorized large city department. (Photos courtesy Seagrave, and National Archives of Canada)

Linfield, Pennsylvania operated this attractive two-tank chemical car. Neither the year nor make is known. It looks like it dates from about 1910. "Linfield" is painted above the radiator and there is an outside chance that this was a very short-lived make of truck. On the side of the seat note hand-activated gong and on the running board an acetylene tank for fueling the headlights. On the rear running board behind the wheel is a stack of pails, probably used to help recharge the chemical tanks. (Photo courtesy Limerick Township Historical Society)

This is a 1910 Buckeye chassis outfitted as a pumper by Howe for use as Engine 10 in Patterson, New Jersey. Pump is at rear. (Photo courtesy Dick Adelman)

The circa-1910 chief's buggy was a Stanley Steamer runabout, one of the better-known makes of steam-powered autos. From left to right we see a hanging Dietz lantern, a fire extinguisher, and a bell. Horizontal tank on running board is for acetylene to power headlights. (Photo courtesy Robert Randlett)

An unidentified salvage corps truck, carrying a crew of eleven, circa 1910. (Photo courtesy The New Jersey Historical Society, Cone Collection)

This is a circa-1910 Webb combination pump and hose car with a piston pump. It carries a long, preconnected squirrel tail hard suction hose. Note dog behind driver. The truck is riding on Firestone pneumatic tires and carries a spare tire, rare for fire apparatus. This picture was originally taken for use in tire advertising. (Photo courtesy Firestone Archives)

In a scene played throughout North America, motorized apparatus replaced horses. In Akron, Ohio, a circa-1910 Webb on a Thomas Flyer chassis shows up to replace one of the pieces of horse-drawn apparatus. (Photo courtesy University of Akron Archives)

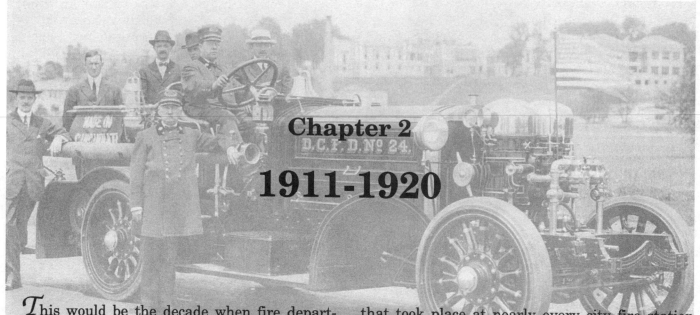

Chapter 2
1911-1920

*T*his would be the decade when fire departments switched to motorized apparatus. Almost no horse-drawn equipment would be purchased. Considerable sales were made of motorized tractors to take the place of horses in front of steam pumps and ladder trucks. The replacement of the horses was a traumatic experience for firefighters and fire buffs. Fire horses had always received loving care. They were exercised daily. In cold weather, after racing to the fire, the horses would be covered with blankets to reduce the possibility of chills. If the apparatus was placed in service at the fire site, the horses would be unhitched and walked to allow them to cool off. After returning to quarters, the horses would be rubbed until they were dry, and their feet would be washed and examined for stones or loose nails.

The horses had been faithful and had shared the dangers and the excitement. Motorized apparatus were noisy, initially undependable, and had an almost comic appearance. In their early days, they were difficult to start, and horse-drawn apparatus would be speeding toward the fire while the motorized apparatus were being cranked. Their introduction signaled an end to a near-romantic era of fire fighting.

The advantage of motorized apparatus was cost. Fewer stations were needed because horses could only pull heavy apparatus at top speed for distances of about one-half mile. Motorized apparatus had no similar limitation. Horses consumed feed every day, while motorized rigs consumed fuel only while in use. And so, in a sad ceremony that took place at nearly every city fire station throughout the nation, fire horses were retired.

FDNY bought a gasoline-propelled Nott streamer and a Waterous pump in 1911, although neither worked out in a satisfactory manner. They also purchased some Christie tractors, used to take the place of horses in front of existing apparatus. Several motorized hose wagons and combination chemical/hose wagons were also purchased. "At the beginning of motorization a problem developed. It was taking units longer to 'turn out' of quarters due to the time lost in hand cranking the motors. Apparently, the horses could be harnessed and on their way more quickly. One engine company built an inclined ramp in quarters and backed the [motorized] steamer up onto it. When an alarm was received, the chauffeur would roll the apparatus down the ramp in gear with the clutch depressed and release it to start the engine."[1] In 1913 FDNY made its last purchase of horses. In 1914 FDNY purchased forty-two Christie tractors and two Garford tractors, with the latter two used to take the place of horses to pull water towers. By 1915 senior officers were reluctant to motorize further because of frequent breakdowns of motorized rigs en route to fires.

The major development in apparatus was the acceptance of motorized rigs that used the same engine for both propulsion and for pumping water. Later, the truck's power takeoff would be harnessed so it could raise an aerial ladder. Both developments represent an advancement over the practice of merely buying a motorized tractor to

---

[1] John A. Calderone and Jack Lerch. *Wheels of the Bravest, a History of FDNY Fire Apparatus, 1865-1982* (Howard Beach, NY: 1984), pp. 56 and 58.

take the place of horses in moving the apparatus to the fire. As departments motorized, they kept expense records of motorized equipment, comparing it with expenses of maintaining horses. In late 1918 the chief at Waltham, Massachusetts, reported the following:

> We now have in service eight pieces of motor apparatus which cover the work formerly done by 18 horses. The cost of maintenance of this apparatus for the year 1918 will be under $1,000. With the present price of hay and oats, the cost of maintenance of 18 horses for the year 1918 would be about $4,500, a conservative estimate of only $250 per horse. . . .
>
> The saving over horse-drawn apparatus is a big item, but the great benefit to our city is in the quickness of response to fires; the running time is cut down over one-half in responding to alarms with the motor apparatus. In the last seven years several instances have been noted of the saving of valuable property in the outlying sections of the city by the quick response of the apparatus.[2]

A related report from Wilkes-Barre, Pennsylvania, indicated that motorized apparatus also freed up firefighters at the scene of the fire: "With the horse-drawn steam engine a driver was needed [who would care for the horses at the fire site], also an engineer to take care of the engine, and a stoker to keep the fire up. With the motor apparatus, the chauffeur runs the engine and the pump, and the other two men are free to fight the fire . . . ."[3]

Solid, hard-riding rubber tires were common on apparatus. (In 1915 the Dayton Rubber Company released copies of a letter from the Pomona Fire Chief correcting erroneous reports that "have been circulated to the effect that our American-LaFrance Type 12 pumping engine, which is equipped with Dayton airless tires, had thrown a tire while en route to a fire . . . ."[4]) Pneumatic tires were used only on autos and at this early time were very undependable.

This was also the decade when salvage corps switched to motorized equipment. In Albany in 1912, the Albany Fire Protectives purchased a 1912 Oldsmobile chassis upon which a salvage body chassis was mounted. In 1915 the Baltimore Fire Insurance Salvage Corps bought an American-LaFrance, the cost of which was partially offset by the sale of four horses and two wagons. Later in the decade, the Baltimore group completed their motorization by buying Packards and Whites. Boston's corps added some Whites to its fleet of Knoxes, and Chicago's corps bought a fleet of Whites. In 1911 the Milwaukee Fire Insurance Patrol put a Knox into operation, in 1912, a Stegeman, and in 1916, a REO. The Insurance Patrol in New Orleans bought a 1912 Knox. In early 1910 the New York Fire Patrol motorized. "A Knox auto was purchased for the Superintendent, and in July, a Knox truck chassis was bought on which a body from one of the horse-drawn wagons was mounted. . . ."[5] The Underwriters Fire Patrol in San Francisco bought some American-LaFrance rigs in 1911. The Fire Insurance Patrol in St. Paul bought a 1910 Waterous.

This was a busy and formative time for many apparatus manufacturers. Ahrens-Fox experimented with several pumpers including a rig with a small front-mount Hale 250 gpm pump. In 1913 Ahrens-Fox introduced what would become its famous front-mount model, initially with two domes, and then one. The pumper came in two versions: one had a compartment for hose, the other carried no hose but devoted the space to bench seats for firefighters. In 1914 Ahrens-Fox also stopped building steam pumpers. The Ahrens-Fox pumper with its distinctive single polished globe for several decades became the single apparatus most associated with large city fire departments. Tales of its outperforming other makes of pumpers are legendary. Both four-cylinder and six-cylinder engines were used, with the latter requiring a distinctly longer hood. The piston pump performed well, although eventually the much simpler centrifugal pumps used by competitors would win out.

American-LaFrance was building both commercial trucks and fire apparatus, and by 1914 decided to concentrate on fire apparatus only. The firm built its last steam pumper in 1914. They were also doing a thriving business outfitting Ford Model Ts with twin chemical tanks and selling them to small-town fire departments and to the War Department for protecting Army camps. During the decade, American-LaFrance supplied many cities with ladder trucks, rotary-gear pump-

[2] *The American City* (December 1918), p. 477.

[3] *The American City* (June 1919), p. 576.

[4] *The American City* (July 1915), p. 79.

[5] Emmons E. Douglass. *While the Flames Raged* (Middletown, NY: 1993), p. 149.

ers, and chemical rigs. In terms of numbers, they would probably be the leading supplier of custom equipment until the 1960s or 1970s.

Boyd continued in business supplying both custom apparatus and equipment to be placed on other makes of chassis. In 1912 FDNY purchased twenty Macks that had chemical and hose bodies supplied by Boyd. Boyd's sales were mainly in the East. The firm dropped out of business toward the end of the decade.

Christie's tractor delivered to FDNY in 1911 had a 90 horsepower, 4-cylinder engine mounted ahead of the axle, and the road wheels were powered by meshed gear wheels inside them. The tractor had a turntable to which the apparatus was attached, and the turntable could pivot within its own length. By 1918 Christie had built over six hundred of these tractors, with nearly a third going to FDNY. During World War I, the firm's interest switched to building tanks and other vehicles for the army. Production of Christie front drive tractors for fire apparatus switched to Wedlake-Lamson Co. of Hoboken.

Four Wheel Drive Auto Company was founded in Clintonville, Wisconsin, in 1912. Its unique product was a device for powering the front steering axle. This, in addition to a conventional rear axle, gave the truck much better traction. This added traction made FWD a popular choice for outfitting apparatus pumps and bodies built by others. At this time FWD marketed apparatus under its own name. Minneapolis purchased an early FWD with a combination chemical and hose body, using it to pull a steamer.

In Kansas City, Missouri, the George C. Hale Company was started. In 1913 the firm delivered a motorized rig to Tulsa. Shortly thereafter, large orders were received from Kansas City, Missouri, and Pittsburgh.

Howe sold numerous horse-drawn, gasoline-powered pumpers before World War I. In 1915 the firm delivered an "automobile pumper" to Lutherville, Maryland. In 1917 the firm moved from Indianapolis to Anderson, Indiana. They did this in order to be closer to the firm producing Lambert automobiles, the chassis of which were used for Howe apparatus. During World War I, they delivered 163 pumpers to the government to protect military bases.

Knox fire apparatus continued to be popular. Charles Hay Martin joined the firm as chief engineer. Martin invented a fifth wheel device for attaching apparatus trailers, and the firm soon began to market Knox-Martin tractors. That market was short-lived and the firm would drop out of business in 1923.

Maxim began building fire apparatus that were sold in New England. In 1915 the firm's first pumper was on a Thomas Flyer auto chassis, and used a Rumsey rotary gear pump. In 1917 the firm delivered a single-bank city service truck to Winthrop, Massachusetts. In 1918 the firm's name became Maxim Motor Company.

The W. S. Nott Company of Minneapolis continued to manufacture and sell gigantic pumpers to an impressive list of customers. Some owners had problems with them; in Oakland, firefighters called their unit the "Nott Go Pumper."

In Appleton, Wisconsin, Humphrey Pierce and his son Dudley founded The Auto Body Works to build bodies for autos (which was a common practice at that time) and buses and trucks. Much later in the century the firm would evolve into one of the nation's largest suppliers of fire apparatus.

In 1912 Pirsch delivered to an Illinois community a hose wagon mounted on a Jeffrey chassis. In 1916, using a White chassis, the firm built a pumper for Creston, Iowa. They also built a chemical and hose unit for Niles, Illinois, using a White chassis.

Pope Hartford specialized in chemical cars, hose wagons, and combination chemical-hose wagons. The purchaser had the choice of Champion or Holloway chemical tanks. The firm was also well known for its productions of ambulances and police "paddy" wagons. The firm dropped out of business just before World War I.

Robinson Fire Apparatus of St. Louis made a number of deliveries during the decade. In 1917 the firm delivered six 700 gpm pumpers to FDNY. Other major cities with Robinson apparatus were Boston; Canton; Detroit; Lansing; Los Angeles; Morristown, New Jersey; Sioux City, Iowa; St. Louis; Wilmington, Delaware; and Youngstown.

Seagrave worked in conjunction with the Gorham Engineering Company of Oakland to use Gorham pumps and engines on their apparatus. Early sales of the Seagrave/Gorhams were to Oakland and Pasadena, California. A total of forty-one Seagrave/Gorham deliveries were made. Seagrave also acquired rights to use a centrifugal pump built by Manistee Iron Works of Manistee, Michigan (which had acquired rights from the English developer). Many orders were received and the Gorham association appeared to vanish. During this same decade, Seagrave sold chemical and hose wagons, city service, and straight-frame and two-piece aerial ladders. In 1915 Chicago purchased the first of a fleet of fifty Seagrave 750 gpm centrifugal pumpers, some of which were to remain in service until the early 1950s. In this era Seagrave was probably the best-known producer of ladder trucks, and turned out trucks on both straight and tractor/trailer chassis. Seagrave also manufactured two-wheel and four-wheel tractors to take the place of horses in front of older rigs.

For part of the decade covered here, Waterous built its own apparatus. New York City, Bridgeport, Cleveland, and Seattle were all early Waterous customers. About 1918 the firm decided to use chassis provided by other builders and to supply their pumps to other makers of fire apparatus.

Before World War I, Webb apparatus were proving to be very popular and by 1914 they were being used in over one hundred different communities. Two criticisms were that the apparatus was top-heavy and that repair parts were difficult to obtain. Suddenly, there was no mention of the firm. An ad was spotted that said James Boyd & Bro. were manufacturing and selling Webb apparatus under the personal supervision of A. C. Webb. But, as mentioned above, the Boyd firm itself was also out of business by the decade's end.

White trucks, built for many years in Cleveland, were a distinguished make of commercial truck and were widely used in the fire fighting service. A number of apparatus outfitters used White chassis for pumpers or for ladder trucks. White tractors were often purchased to replace horses or earlier tractors. At the time of World War I, White was also marketing its own line of pumpers and ladder trucks, and received a major order from the army to build fire trucks used in military camps.

A new municipal problem was adapting traffic rules and procedures that allowed the freer movement of fire apparatus and other emergency vehicles. There also had to be rules regarding the "safe" driving of fire apparatus. In 1919 a "survey of the regulations regarding the speed of motor fire apparatus in all parts of the United States shows that the maximum speed permitted for heavier pieces of apparatus is between 20 and 25 miles an hour, with some exceptions, allowing as much as 30 miles an hour for the chemical apparatus."[6] In some large cities, the intersections along the main routes from downtown fire stations were equipped with combinations of Klaxon horns and semaphores (similar to those used by railroads) to announce the approaching apparatus. The signs were activated from central headquarters by the dispatcher, who estimated the time it would take the apparatus to reach each intersection. In Portland, Oregon:

The railway type of semaphore was adopted because of its reliability. We have installed the motor-driven, two-position upper right hand quadrant type with a six-foot blade having the word "fire" painted on it. . . . . Attached to the edge of the blade are eight 20-Watt ruby incandescent electric lamps, which are lighted only when the blade reaches a horizontal position. The signals are attached to iron poles at such height that with the blade extended horizontally they are 19 feet above the ground. The gongs are 14-inch motor-driven devices, which operate when the lamps are lighted and make sufficient noise to attract the attention of vehicular traffic and motormen in enclosed cars.[7]

Apparatus of this era used foot-activated gongs or hand-cranked sirens; however, the main sound came from the motorized apparatus themselves: they had no mufflers, which meant that they roared. A refinement was the use of exhaust whistles that worked by having the engine's exhaust feed through a whistle, making a stuttering, screeching sound that came close to waking the dead.

In northern climates it was necessary for cities to buy equipment to plow snow and to keep streets open so they could be used by emergency vehicles during and after snowstorms. Horses had better traction in snow than did many motor vehicles. For a brief period, some cities outfitted some fire apparatus with snowplow blades, but soon responsibility for snow clearance was given to cities' departments of public works.

As communities grew, it was necessary to expand their water supply and distribution systems as well. The National Board of Fire Underwriters, who "rated" communities' fire fighting capacity as a determinant of fire insurance premiums, had recommended standards for water supply. Volume of water and the pressure at which it was available were equally important factors, although one of the functions of the pumper was to increase pressure at the fire site so that it could be effectively used to combat the blaze. According to the Underwriters, in 1919 a city of 1,000 was expected to have a water supply capability of 1000 gallons per minute; a city of 10,000 needed 3000 gallons per minute; a city of 100,000 needed 9,000 gallons per minute; and so on. Recommended pressures at hydrants varied with density and

[6] *The American City* (July 1919), p. 50.
[7] *The American City* (July 1919), p. 52.

height of buildings in the area the hydrant served. Cities located on level terrain would need more pumping capacity to maintain pressures at hydrants than would cities located in hilly or mountainous areas where large reservoirs could be located at higher elevations. The design of each system was unique in terms of having the capability to replace the volume of water and maintain pressure at the same time as the fire department was pumping numerous streams of water at a major conflagration. Part of the cost of water distribution also dealt with the number of hydrants. This is important because water flowing through hoses is hampered by friction.

> When a 1-1/2-inch stream flows from a smooth-bore nozzle, with 100 feet of hose it is possible to throw a stream of 250 gallons per minute 67 feet high; with 200 feet of hose this is reduced to 222 gallons per minute thrown 59 feet high; with 400 feet of hose it is reduced to 188 gallons per minute thrown 44 feet high. . . ; and with 1,000 feet of hose it is reduced to 140 gallons per minute thrown only 25 feet high.[8]

Another network that was related to fire protection was the fire alarm system, consisting of alarm boxes in large buildings and at many intersections, connected by electric wire. To report a fire, one would activate the alarm and wait for fire apparatus to arrive at that point. In large cities there were separate trucks and crews that maintained extensive alarm systems. (At one time Detroit had 700 miles of wire and 3,800 poles to maintain;[9] and Boston had 1,360 fire alarm boxes.[10]) Stations were also linked by telegraphic means. The need for alarm boxes would diminish as use of telephones spread.

---

[8] *The American City* (September 1919), p.243.
[9] *The American City* (August 1922), p. 117.
[10] *The American City* (October 1926), p. 543.

This is a high pressure hose wagon with a large turret pipe on a 1911 Knox chassis. This is one of five used by the Fire Department of New York. (Photo courtesy National Automotive History Collection, Detroit Public Library)

In 1911 Mack built its first pumper using a Mack Senior chassis and a Gould's pump. This one went to the Union Fire Association near Philadelphia. A local carriage maker completed the bodywork. (Photo courtesy Mack)

A 1911 Nott propelled by a gasoline motor and carrying a steam-powered Nott second-size 700 gpm water pump. (Photo courtesy *Fireman's World*)

This photo was taken in New York City during the transition period to motorized apparatus. In the background is Engine 39's 1911 Waterous, with a 750 gpm steam pump. Closer is a horse-drawn pump with blankets protecting the horses as they patiently wait for the fire to be over.

A circa-1911 Packard squad car in Detroit. The rig carried a "flying squad" of additional firefighters to the fire site. (Photo courtesy Len Williams)

Two pictures of Boise's 1911 Seagrave, sixty-five-foot aerial ladder truck, powered by a Miller air-cooled engine. In the picture with the ladder raised, note how the tiller steering wheel is moved to the side. (Photos courtesy Wayne Sorensen Collection)

A 1911 Thomas Flyer chassis used by Webb to build a combination hose and pumper for the Mercer Engine Company of Princeton, New Jersey. (Photo courtesy Charles E. Beckwith)

Seattle purchased three Waterous hose wagons in 1911. This one was assigned to Engine 14. It was powered by a 101 hp Waterous engine and had a forty-gallon chemical tank. (Photo courtesy Dick Schneider Collection)

The first motorized pumper delivered to FDNY was this 750 gpm Waterous, delivered in 1911.

This 1911 3/4-ton White was used as a chief's buggy in Montgomery, Alabama. To the right of the front fender one can see an electric siren. Along the running board appears to be a foot-powered gong. The rear seat is on a tool box and two chemical extinguishers are carried at the rear. Above the fire station door is the wording: "Mechanics H & L Co. No. 1." (Photo courtesy Volvo/White)

MOTOR FIRE APPARATUS

Combination Chemical and Hose Wagons
Pumping Engines

High Pressure Hose Wagons
Hook and Ladder Trucks

Any city can save thousands of dollars to its property owners by installing our motor-propelled fire apparatus—little fires are prevented from becoming big ones; a minute may save the city.

International Motor Trucks

Proved by Years of Successful Service

Mack 12 years in use Saurer 18 years in use Hewitt 10 years in use

You want excellence at two points when you select a motor-propelled fire-fighting apparatus: **time-proved fire apparatus equipment, time-proved chassis.**

Our trucks have withstood all sorts of time tests all over the the world in 10, 12, 18 years of service.

Our apparatus is constructed upon the engineering designs of veteran fire-fighters and veteran apparatus builders.

35 of our trucks purchased by the New York Fire Department

The requirements of the New York board of engineers were peculiarly exacting.

The truck must be susceptible to quick starting; instant control in congested thoroughfares; high and long-continued speed over long, open avenues; and absolute dependability over all conditions of roadway in all weathers, no matter how severe the strain.

You should know what these specifications embody. Let us send you them, and photographs and descriptions of our apparatus.

INTERNATIONAL MOTOR COMPANY

General Offices: Broadway and 57th Street, New York City

This ad appeared in *Firemen's Herald* circa 1912. It was placed by the International Motor Company, which built Hewitt, Mack, and Saurer trucks. Eventually, it would build only Macks.

Chicago's Engine 38 with a circa-1912 Ahrens-Fox Continental 2nd Style 700 gpm fire engine installed upon a 1917 White TAD chain-drive tractor. Note firefighters sitting on the steamer's front seat, and the foot-operated gong beneath it. (Photo courtesy Volvo/White)

This ad shows one of four 1912 Couple Gear electric trucks outfitted with Webb bodies for FDNY. Three of the aerials were seventy-five feet long, and one was eighty-five feet. The rigs were slow moving on streets and soon were placed into reserve status.

New Christie

FRONT DRIVE TRACTORS

FOR

Steam Fire Engines Aerial Trucks and Water Towers

Now Being Manufactured

BY THE

Wedlake-Lamson Co.

HOBOKEN - NEW JERSEY

An ad for Christie Front Drive Tractors to pull steam fire engines, aerial trucks, and water towers. The ad appeared in *Firemen's Herald*.

Chicago's Engine 120 ran this hose wagon built in 1912 by Harder Truck Company of Chicago, a subsidiary of Harder Storage & Van Co. This rig has a chemical tank, windshield, and hard rubber tires. (Photo courtesy Chicago Architectural Photographing Company [John Doyle Collection])

Trenton, New Jersey, purchased this piston pumper in 1912. Howe adapted a Lambert auto chassis. (Photo courtesy Dick Adelman)

A 1912 Mack AB that was converted in 1918 to a fuel wagon by the Baltimore Fire Department. Baskets carry coal for steam pumpers. (Photo courtesy Wayne Sorensen Collection)

A Boyd body was on this 1912 Mack chassis, one of twenty-one ordered by FDNY. These combination chemical and hose wagons were called "Scouts." Note that the driver is not uniformed; he is a paid chauffeur. The picture is posed, as the truck is not moving. (Photo courtesy Gus Johnson)

Chicago's first motorized apparatus was this 1912 Universal Nott with a 900 gpm pump. It ran as Engine 94. (Photo courtesy Chicago Architectural Photographing Co. [John Doyle Collection])

W. S. Nott Company of Minneapolis built this 1912 500 gpm piston pumper for use in Cleveland, Ohio. (Photo courtesy Wayne Sorensen Collection)

Here's a 1912 Pope-Hartford chemical car used in San Francisco. It has two eighty-gallon chemical tanks and an adapter for filling tanks with water at hydrants. (Photo courtesy San Francisco Fire Department)

Here is a 1912 Robinson "Monarch" pumper and hose wagon used by Engine 50 in St. Louis. The squirrel-tail hose is preconnected to the pump. (Photo courtesy T. Stroup Collection)

The Robinson Fire Apparatus Manufacturing Company was located in St. Louis. In 1912 they built this "Jumbo" 2nd size 700 gpm piston pumper for Los Angeles, where it ran as Engine 26. It was the first motorized pumper in Los Angeles. The power plant was a 110 hp Buffalo marine engine. (Photo courtesy Robinson Fire Apparatus Company)

The Webb Fire Apparatus Company used a 1912 Thomas Flyer chassis to mount a 650 gpm Rumsey pump and hose body for use by the Chicago Fire Department. It was that city's first motorized pump and hose combination. Note bell tower in front, common to Chicago apparatus for years. (Photo courtesy Chicago Architectural Photographing Co. [John Doyle Collection])

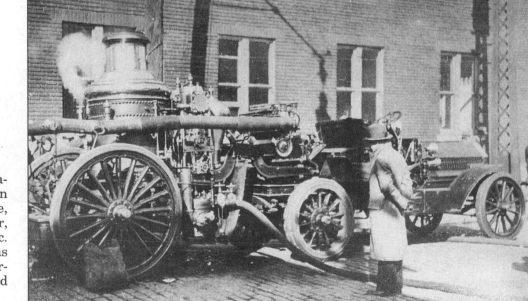

Two views of a 1912 Seagrave tractor installed in front of a Waterous, 1st size, 900 gpm steam pumper, used in Montreal, Quebec. The view from the front was taken in 1931. (Photos courtesy Wayne Sorensen and Dick Adelman)

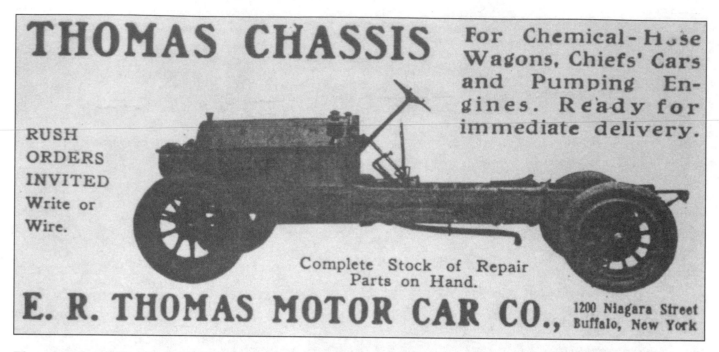

Thomas automobiles, especially their "Flyer," were well-known before World War I. Here's an ad the firm ran circa 1912, indicating that they supplied chassis for "chemical-hose wagons, chiefs' cars, and pumping engines."

The United Fire Company No. 3 of Frederick, Maryland, operated this 1912 500 gpm Waterous triple combination. It carried a chemical tank. Power was provided by a 101 hp water-cooled engine equipped with a Stromberg carburetor and a dual electrical ignition system.

A 1912 Webb Couple Gear two-wheel tractor installed in front of FDNY's Engine 217's 1907 Nott, 1st size, 900 gpm steam pumper. (Photo courtesy Gus Johnson)

This 1910 American-LaFrance sixty-five-foot water tower was raised by spring action. Used in Philadelphia, it is shown being pulled by a 1912 Webb-Couple Gear electric tractor. A deck gun is visible above the rear wheel. In 1922 the electric tractor was replaced by a Seagrave tractor. Electric tractors were slow and needed to be towed when they ran out of electricity.

Youngstown, Ohio's first motorized rig was this circa-1912 Webb, which had been built on a Thomas touring car chassis. Note that the preconnected suction hose carried squirrel-tail style. (Photo courtesy Wayne Sorensen)

In front of Baltimore's main fire station in 1913 we see a mix of horse-drawn and motorized apparatus. From left is Engine 32's horse-drawn steamer, a Holloway combination hose wagon, a 1909 White chief's buggy, a 1913 Mack AB high pressure wagon, and a horse-drawn Hays aerial ladder. (Photo courtesy Gus Johnson)

Portland, Oregon, purchased this 1913 American-LaFrance Type 12 combination 700 gpm pump and hose car in service as Engine 17. Headlights and floodlight are fueled with acetylene. Tires have virtually no tread. The chains were used for traction on dirt streets.

This 1913 Ahrens-Fox Model B 700 gpm piston pumper was used in Washington, D.C., running as Engine 24, and accompanied by a hose wagon carried on a White chassis. The banner in the rear says: "Made in Cincinnati." In the pumper's truck bed were seats for the firefighters. (Photo courtesy Dick Adelman)

This is one of the six 1913 American-LaFrance Type 10 combination chemical and hose cars that Portland, Oregon, purchased. Note especially the lights and the plumbing connections for the twin thirty-five-gallon chemical tanks feeding into the hose reel. (Photo courtesy Oregon Historical Society)

Here we see a 1913 Christie tractor that pulled Toledo's 1897 Champion sixty-five-foot water tower. (Photos courtesy Charles E. Beckwith)

Here are motorized apparatus working at a church fire in New York City. At lower left is a circa-1913 Christie tractor pulling a steamer, and at lower right is a circa-1915 Mack hose wagon. (Photo courtesy Gus Johnson)

This 1913 apparatus consists of a Christie tractor unit joined with an Ahrens-Fox second size, 700 gpm pumper. It had the equivalent of a single, straight frame, and it was used in Somerville, Massachusetts. (Photo courtesy Gus Johnson)

Columbus, Ohio's 1913 Gorham/Seagrave, model 144, 1000 gpm pumper. Pump is at the rear, and only suction hose is carried. (Photo courtesy Seagrave)

A 1913 Kissel chemical car and hose wagon used in Madison, Wisconsin. In its later years it was converted to a foam truck, carrying a foam hopper and canisters of foam. This truck is painted gray; after World War II, Madison painted its apparatus red. In Wisconsin's 1948 Centennial parade the Kissel appeared as Madison's oldest apparatus.

A circa-1913 Knox-Martin three-wheel tractor with a four-cylinder 40 hp engine attached to a Seagrave seventy-five-foot aerial ladder, operated by the Mt. Vernon, New York, Fire Department. Note star above tractor's front wheel. Its purpose was to let the operator know the direction the wheel was pointing. (Photo courtesy Gus Johnson)

Here we see Springfield, Massachusetts' Engine 4, a 1903 American, 2nd size, 700 gpm steamer being pulled by a circa-1913 Knox-Martin three-wheel tractor. (Photo courtesy Gus Johnson)

It was a cold day in New York when this photo was taken. Spray from the deck pipe has frozen. The hose and deluge wagon is one of ten built by Boyd on 1913-14 Mack Senior chassis. The driver's seat is above the engine and front wheels, a carryover from horse-drawn wagons. This wagon ran with a pumper, a 1900 American steamer, pulled by a Christie tractor.

A 1913 Seagrave sidesaddle, straight-frame, tiller, seventy-five-foot aerial. The close-up shows the front driver's seat with limited vision to the driver's left. (Photos courtesy Seagrave)

A 1913 Velie model 40 touring car chassis used by Webb to build a combination chemical and hose car for Kansas City, Missouri. It ran as Hose Company 11, which was manned by blacks. (Photo courtesy Wayne Sorensen Collection)

One of the first uses of motorized apparatus was to rush additional manpower to the fire site, where they would augment crews already attacking the blaze. Large departments had "flying squads" to serve this purpose. This is a 1914 Autocar flying squad. Note bench sets in the center and two eighty-gallon chemical tanks at the rear. There are additional extinguishers on the tailboard. An Autocar ad of this time period said: "Fire-fighting equipment is always ready for call when it is installed on an Autocar chassis." The driver's seat is above and ahead of the motor, an idea that would be reborn thirty years later. (Photo courtesy American Automobile Manufacturers Association)

Louisville's 1892, fifty-five-foot Hale water tower was originally built for New York City by the Kansas City Fire Department Supply Company; however, it was never delivered to New York. It was first shown at the International Association of Fire Engineers convention in Louisville in the Fall of 1892. It was then loaned to the Columbia Exposition fire brigade at the Chicago's World Fair, where it was manned by Chicago Fire Department firefighters. Then it was sold to Louisville. In 1914 Louisville motorized the tower with a one-wheel Autohorse known as "iron mule" tractor, which we see here. The Autohorse was a single-wheel tractor built in St. Louis by the One Wheel Truck Co. Note the flat "buckboard" front end. The tractor had a single pivoting wheel under the driver, with the four-cylinder Continental engine behind the driver. The rear of the tractor's frame was attached to the front of the trailer's frame. The tractor was replaced by a Mack AC tractor in 1919. In 1944 a Chevrolet tractor with a fully enclosed cab replaced the 1919 Mack. The unit was retired in 1966, replaced by a snorkel. (Photo courtesy Caufield & Shook Collection, University of Louisville Photographic Archives)

San Francisco's first motorized pumper was this 1914 Ahrens-Fox, Model B, double dome, 700 gpm unit. It served as San Francisco's Engine 10 for twenty-two years, and was accompanied by a hose wagon. This photo was taken sometime after 1930 when pneumatic tires replaced those of hard rubber. The engine was a 92 hp Herschell-Spillman. (Photo courtesy San Francisco Fire Department)

This is an Ahrens-Fox tractor built in 1914. It was used to replace horses on Sacramento's 1911 Seagrave, eighty-five-foot aerial. (Photo courtesy R. J. Calverton)

A 1914 Couple-Gear with an eighty-five-foot Seagrave aerial ladder, running as Ladder 8 in Springfield, Massachusetts. A gas motor mounted midship supplied electric power for drive units in each wheel. (Photo courtesy Gus Johnson)

Sandusky, Ohio, ran this 1914 Clydesdale combination chemical and hose car, built in Clyde, Ohio. (Photo courtesy Wayne Sorensen Collection)

The Seattle department's shop mated a 1907 American-LaFrance Metropolitan 2nd size, 700 gpm steam pumper to a 1914 Christie two-wheel tractor. The tractor was powered by a 48 hp engine. This pumper ran as part of Engine 14, accompanied by a hose wagon. Note the apron on the steamer in front of the firebox: it was to catch sparks and cinders. (Photo courtesy Dick Schneider)

A 1914 FWD with a 500 gpm Northern rotary pump, used by Mountain Iron, Wisconsin. It had a forty-gallon chemical tank. (Photo courtesy FWD)

In 1914 Minneapolis purchased this FWD, which was equipped as a combination chemical and hose wagon body. Its added duty was to pull Engine 5's Clapp & Jones 1893 800 gpm steam pumper. Note right-hand steering and radiator cover. (Photo courtesy Minneapolis Fire Department)

A Thomas Flyer chassis was used by Maxim to carry this 1914 Maxim chemical and hose car. It was used in Ansonia, Connecticut. (Photo courtesy Dick Adelman Collection)

This 1914 Maxim chemical and hose unit was delivered to Middleboro, Massachusetts. (Photo courtesy Maxim)

Springfield, Massachusetts, bought this 1914 Nott 700 gpm pumper that also carried a chemical tank, making it a triple combination.

New Brunswick, New Jersey, ran this circa-1914 Robinson city service truck. It carried a full complement of ladders, the longest being fifty-five feet. (Photo courtesy Robinson Fire Apparatus Company)

The NEW "UNIVERSAL"

SIX CYLINDER
COMBINATION CHEMICAL ENGINE AND HOSE WAGON

FIRST OF THE FIRST CLASS

"Universal" Combination Chemical-Hose Car

SOME POINTS OF EXCELLENCE

NINETY Horse Power

SPEED—70 miles an hour

5 PER CENT NICKEL STEEL in transmission and crank shaft.

HOSE CAPACITY   2,500 feet

Solid tires unless otherwise ordered

Full Details Promptly Furnished

NOTT FIRE ENGINE COMPANY, Minneapolis, Minn.

D. A. WOODHOUSE, General Eastern Agent,   J. L. PHILLIPS, General Pacific Coast Representative, Seattle, Washington.
50 West Broadway, N. Y.

A trade journal ad for a Nott, circa 1914. Note reference to seventy miles per hour speed.

Seattle bought two of these Gorham/Seagraves in 1914. The rear-mounted Gorham pump was rated at 800 gpm. This unit served as Engine 8 and Engine 4, and was retired in 1932. (Photo courtesy R. Dale Magee)

Oklahoma City used this 1914 Thomas Flyer to pull Truck 3's Rumsey city service ladder. For a brief time, Thomas Flyers were very popular with apparatus outfitters. This one had a 48 hp engine. (Photo courtesy Wayne Sorensen)

Bridgeport, Connecticut, used this 1914 Waterous 900 gpm piston pumper as Engine 2. The pump inlet is at the rear of the hose box, and it looks as though the pump itself takes up most of the space behind the seat. The six-cylinder engine produced 101 horsepower. Waterous sold similar equipment to Washington, D.C., New York City, and Richmond. (Photo courtesy Waterous)

This circa-1915 Boyd ad shows a chemical rig delivered to Leominster, Pennsylvania. A Kanawha air-pressure chemical tank was installed by Boyd.

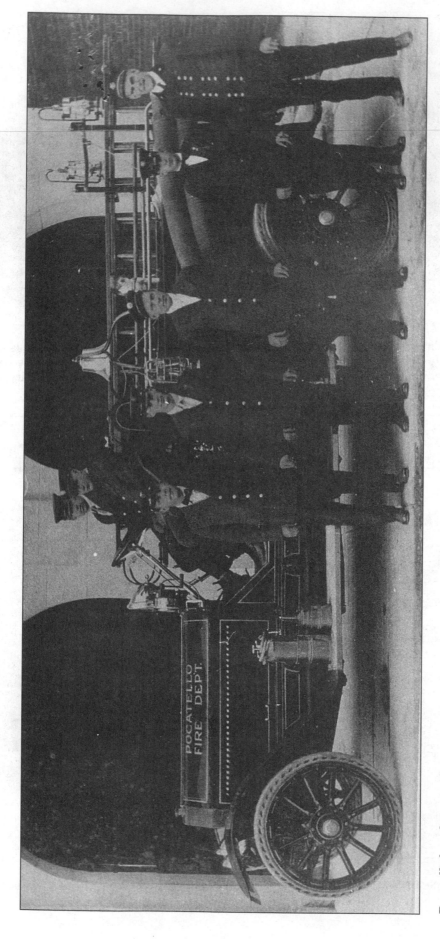

Pocatello bought as its first motorized apparatus this 1915 American-LaFrance Type 12, 1000 gpm pump and hose car. Co-author Sorensen grew up in Pocatello and recalls seeing this engine often. As a young boy Sorensen would visit the fire station and be allowed to wipe the engine down with a soft cloth. On special occasions, he'd be allowed to help polish the engine, ring the bell, and turn the siren's crank. For the 4th of July parade, a brace of American flags would be placed around the radiator cap. Note the pattern of holes in the solid rubber tires: they were supposed to give a cushioning effect. At the right is the chief engineer with two rows of nine brass buttons on his uniform coat. The hosemen had three brass buttons and the callmen had no brass buttons. This engine served until 1946 and is now on display in the Bannock County Museum. (Photo courtesy Bannock County Historical Museum)

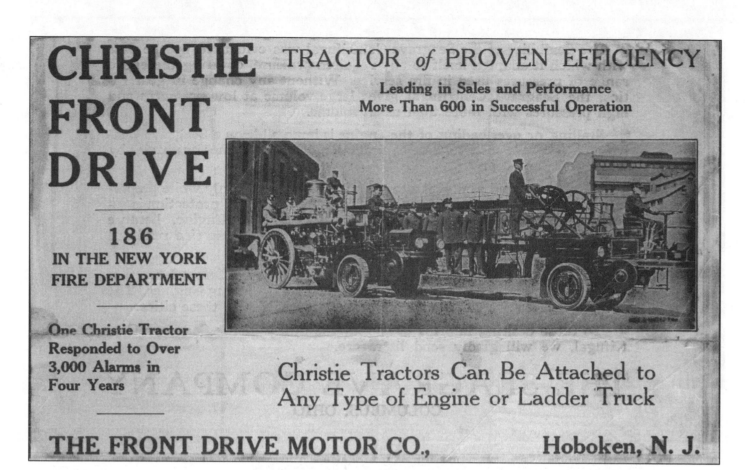
A *Firemen's Herald* ad proclaims that 186 Christie front drive tractors were used by FDNY.

The Underwriters Salvage Corps in St. Louis used this 1915 Dorris two-ton salvage rig. The Dorris Motor Car Company was also located in that city. (Photo courtesy Robert Pauly)

This 1897 Champion sixty-five-foot water tower was operated in Toledo. In 1915 a Christie front wheel tractor was purchased to substitute for horses. The rig is currently in the Hall of Flame Museum in Phoenix. At bottom left is an outrider jack. At the base of the tower we see a hand crank for lifting the tower. A deck nozzle has been placed above the driver's seat. Below the letters "TFD" is large flywheel, and at the top of the road wheel is a device that emits a sound as the wheel turns, similar to backup-warning devices used on some trucks today. (Photo courtesy Don Wood)

This is a 1915 Morton two-wheel tractor installed in front of an 1866 Amoskeag 600 gpm pumper, operated by the Union Fire Company of Lebanon, Pennsylvania. Morton Truck and Tractor Co. was located in Harrisburg. (Photo courtesy Morton)

This is a pre-World War I photo taken in front of a New York City fire station. At left is a Boyd hose and chemical wagon on a Mack chassis, one of twenty-nine the FDNY ordered, and known as "Scouts." The top rack holds pompiers (or scaling ladders) that allow one to go up the side of a building by hooking the top of the ladder into an overhead window, climbing up to that window, lifting the ladder, and repeating the operation. Barely visible behind the front bumper is a spring-loaded cranking device to help start the truck more quickly. The center apparatus is Engine 93, an American-LaFrance Metropolitan 2nd size, 700 gpm steam pumper, pulled by a Christie tractor. In the distance is Engine 93's Boyd/Mack hose and chemical wagon.

Chicago's Engine 98 operated this 1916 Ahrens-Fox 750 gpm pumper, one of five purchased. (Photo courtesy Chicago Architectural Photographing Co. [John Doyle Collection])

A 1916 Boyd two-wheel tractor installed in front of Philadelphia's American-LaFrance Metropolitan, 3rd size, 600 gpm pumper. (Photo courtesy Philadelphia Fire Department)

This is Chicago's Engine 62, a 1916 American-LaFrance, Type 12, 750 gpm pumper. The bell is mounted high, in front of the radiator. Just below the seat is a bell-shaped container, which is the air chamber for the rotary gear pump. (Photo courtesy Chicago Architectural Photographing Co. [John Doyle Collection])

Philadelphia ran this attractive 1916 Boyd double tank chemical and hose car, in service at Engine 7. Note large play-pipe carried at the rear. (Photo courtesy Gus Johnson)

This was Ladder 3 in New Bedford, which was installed on a 1916 Couple Gear Electric chassis. The seventy-five-foot aerial was elevated through use of a Dahill air hoist. Note location of tillerman, below the aerial. (Photo courtesy Gus Johnson)

This fire scene in New York City shows, on the left, a circa-1916 Christie tractor linked to Engine 221's steamer, which is pumping water to the turret gun on top of the horse-drawn, high pressure hose wagon on the right. The horses have been unhitched and taken to a drier, safer location. (Photo courtesy Gus Johnson)

A 1916 Gramm Bernstein truck chassis was used to motorize Lima, Ohio's aerial ladder. Note life net.

This 1916 Garford was used in Moore, Pennsylvania. It was outfitted by Boyd, and carries a 350 gpm pump. (Photo courtesy Paul Darrell Collection)

Hale Motor Fire Apparatus

TYPE 2 COMBINATION CHEMICAL AND HOSE CAR IN SERVICE IN KANSAS CITY, MO.

Motor Pumping Engines and Hose Cars, Motor Service Trucks, Salvage Cars, Chief's or Scout Chemical Cars and Combination Chemical and Hose Motor Cars in three sizes—a light 4 cylinder Combination for the smaller cities as well as Standard 4 and 6 cylinder Combinations.

A CAR FOR EVERY PURPOSE AND CONDITION

The continual excellent service, low upkeep and expressions of satisfaction by all using our apparatus is the best evidence of its superiority. It will be well worth your time to investigate our apparatus thoroughly.

Motor Driven and Horse Drawn Fire Apparatus **THE GEO. C. HALE CO.** General Fire Department Equipment

Office and Factory, 119-21 West 14th Street, KANSAS CITY, MO.

A *Firemen's Herald* Hale ad from before World War I. At bottom left is the statement, "Motor Driven and Horse Drawn Fire Apparatus."

Howe assembled this pumper in 1916—using a Crane-Simplex auto chassis—for Eden, New Jersey. (Photo courtesy Dick Adelman)

Indianapolis operated this 1916 city service truck built on a Kelly chassis. The sloping hood is sometimes referred to as "Renault-style," with fan at the rear.

It was mid-winter when this picture was taken in Boston. Covered with ice is Engine Company 8's 1916 Seagrave 750 gpm centrifugal pumper. (Photo courtesy Gus Johnson)

This is one of two two-wheel tractors built by Seagrave in 1916 and sold to Seattle for installation in front of horse-drawn apparatus. This 73 hp tractor was used to pull Engine 10's 1904 Nott 1st size, 900 gpm pumper, and another was used to pull a 1904 Champion rear-mount sixty-five-foot water tower. (Photo courtesy Seagrave)

This 1916 White tractor was used to pull a Chicago Fire Department shop-built city service trailer. A life net is behind the ladder hanging on the left side. Tractors and semi-trailers could often turn in shorter distances than straight trucks since the tractor could be at right angles to the trailer. (Photo courtesy Chicago Architectural Photographing Company [John Doyle Collection])

Firemen in Quebec, in 1917, using a horse-drawn boiler to generate steam needed to thaw frozen hydrants. (Photo courtesy National Archives of Canada)

At left is FDNY's Engine 27, a circa-1917 American-LaFrance Type 75, 700 gpm pumper. On the right is a 1914 Mack/Boyd deluge wagon. The American-LaFrance is supplying both turrets. (Photo courtesy Wayne Sorensen Collection)

The One Wheel Truck Co. of St. Louis delivered six of these Autohorses to that city's fire department in 1917. Only four were placed in use and they proved to be unsatisfactory. They were retired in the late 1920s. They had problems with cobblestones and with snow and ice on streets. In bad weather, companies would leave them and their attached steamer in the station and respond with only their hose wagons. This picture shows two of the tractors. The one on the left is attached to a 1898 American-LaFrance "Metropolitan" 1st size, 900 gpm steam pumper, which ran as Engine 15. On the right is Engine 39, a 1908 American-LaFrance "Metropolitan" 2nd size, 700 gpm steam pumper. (Photo courtesy Paul Nauman)

A 1917 Mack AC carrying a circa-1899 hose box that had originally been on a horse-drawn Holloway combination hose wagon. It ran as High Pressure Unit #3 in Baltimore. It carried three Morse monitor pipes.

Chicago used this 1917 Christie tractor to pull their 1905 American-LaFrance 2nd size, 700 gpm steam pumping engine. The Christie tractor has a transversely-mounted four-cylinder engine. Note that the crank under the number 126 is parallel to the tractor's axle. (Photo courtesy Chicago Architectural Photographing Co. [John Doyle Collection])

Truck 3 in Chicago was this 1917 Mack AC, which pulled a 1903 Seagrave eighty-five-foot aerial ladder that had initially been horse-drawn. Unusual is the chain guard in front of the tractor's rear wheels. (Photo courtesy Chicago Architectural Photographing Co. and John Doyle)

Detroit used this 1917 Seagrave 750 gpm pumper. Note details of chain drive. (Photo courtesy Seagrave and Dick Adelman)

Boston used this 1917 Seagrave as its Combination Chemical and Hose Car Wagon # 8. The four-cylinder motor produced 52 horsepower and came with a Westinghouse self-starter. A thirty-gallon copper chemical tank was under the seat. (Photo courtesy Seagrave and Dick Adelman)

Here we see a 1917 Van Bierk two-wheel tractor that was installed in front of FDNY's 1909 American-LaFrance, 2nd size, "Metropolitan" 700 gpm steam fire engine. Note the captain riding at the rear of the engine.

Seagrave /Water Tower, St. Paul, Minn.

553

St. Paul used this 1917 Seagrave chain drive, sixty-five-foot water tower. The tower was spring-raised; the spring compression cylinders are visible at rear. The windshield is divided, with half on each side of the lowered tower. A deck gun is barely visible between the two central firemen. (Photo courtesy Wright State University)

An ad from about the time of World War I indicating the Webb apparatus were "now manufactured and sold by the Boyd firm. The partnership arrangement was apparently not of the "win-win" variety, since soon the Boyd firm also dropped out of business.

A 1918 American-LaFrance Type 31 two-wheel tractor designed to take the place of horses. It is powered by a four-cylinder, 75 hp engine. This one was used in Boise as Engine 1 and is shown attached to a 1912 1st size, 900 gpm American-LaFrance steam fire engine. In the background is a 1964 American-LaFrance 900 Series, 1000 gpm pumper. (Photo courtesy Wayne Sorensen)

In 1918 Chevrolet became part of General Motors, and also began producing trucks. In that same year one of the early Chevrolet trucks went to Sudbury, Ontario, where it was coupled with a non-tillered Seagrave city service truck. The Chevrolet's headlights were mounted on the cowl and there was a hand-cranked siren.

Here is a 1918 Dodge/Pirsch used by the U.S. Army. Built on a half-ton chassis, the rig carries a chemical tank and hose, and two Pyrene extinguishers. (Photo courtesy Dick Adelman)

Jacob Press Body Co. of Chicago built hose bodies for two-piece engine companies. This one was mounted on a 1918 Ford TT chassis. Note the foot-operated gong, and the hard tires in the rear. Windshields were uncommon on apparatus at this time. (Photo courtesy Chicago Architectural Photographing Co. [John Doyle Collection])

Pirsch used some 1918 Ford TT chassis to build hose wagons for Chicago. Note pneumatic tires in front and solid tires in rear. (Photo courtesy Chicago Architectural Photographing Company [John Doyle Collection])

The army bought fire apparatus during World War I and here we see a 1918 Ford with a roadster body and lengthened chassis at a motor park in St. Nazaire, France. The frame was extended using a Lambert extension kit. A Buckeye piston pump with a copper tank and a preconnected hard suction hose can all be noted. On the rear step is a Pyrene fire extinguisher. (Photo courtesy National Archives)

This 1918 Kissel carried two chemical tanks. It was used as Chemical 3 in Fresno, California. It was rebuilt by two firemen in a blacksmith shop after being badly damaged in a barn fire.

New Britain, Connecticut, ran this 1918 Maxim Model 615 Hose Wagon. Note canvas windshield. Headlights are not original. (Photo courtesy George E. Warren)

Originally, this 1918 Mack AC was a ladder tractor, but in the 1920s the Chicago Fire Department shops converted it to a combination turret and hose wagon used by High Pressure Company No. 6. (Photo courtesy Dick Adelman)

This is Baltimore's Second Line Truck 11, a 1918 Mack pulling a 1909 Hays eighty-five-foot aerial ladder. It utilizes a modified Dahill air hoist to lift the ladder. Note life net. (Photo courtesy John J. Robrecht)

In 1918 Pirsch used a Winton commercial chassis to build a combination chemical and hose car for Grand Haven, Michigan. (Photo courtesy Dick Adelman)

One of many Whites delivered to the War Department during World War I. This chemical and hose rig was used at Fort Leavenworth. (Photo courtesy Library of Congress)

This cartoon ran in the November 1919 issue of *The American City* and showed how cities were using motorized equipment and better water systems to improve their fire-fighting capability. Reproduced with permission.

HAHN TRIPLE COMBINATION

Hahn literature, circa 1919, showed this triple combination with a Northern rotary gear pump and twin Holloway chemical tanks.

Wellesley, Massachusetts, used this 1919 Maxim city service truck. Ladders are carried in a single bank. (Photo courtesy Dick Adelman Collection)

Baltimore's City Service Truck 24, on a 1919 Mack AC chassis, has been restored and is in the Hall of Flame Museum in Phoenix. The Mack chassis was outfitted with what had been a 1886 Holloway city service truck with two thirty-five-gallon chemical tanks.

Holloway Chemical tanks on the Baltimore Mack. The Holloway tanks are identifiable because of the hood at the top center. Here the tanks are loaded with a water and soda mixture, and the cap is then tightened down. Acid is placed in an upright cup above the mixture and the cup is tipped from outside, adding acid to the mixture. The cranks in the center are used to agitate the mixture. Pipes lead to the hose basket. Hose is coiled left to right, which tends to tighten hose couplings as hose is pulled from the basket. Only one tank would operate at a time; the other would be recharged. A small supply of water was required for recharging, as well as additional chemicals.

A life net carried on the Baltimore Mack. Toward front, note the bell holder.

A 1919 straight-frame, tillered, sixty-five-foot Seagrave aerial with driver's seat in sidesaddle position, which had very poor visibility. This one went to Santa Barbara. It has a chemical tank and hose reel at the rear. (Photo courtesy Seagrave and FWD)

The fire department in Valdosta, Georgia, loaned out two pieces of apparatus to help promote a 1922 movie named *The Still Alarm*. At left is a 1914 American-LaFrance Type 14 city service truck with a forty-gallon chemical tank, and on the right is a 1920 American-LaFrance 750 gpm triple combination pumper, also with a forty-gallon chemical tank. (Photo courtesy Lowndes County Historical Society)

Mack ACs used as fire pumpers had their cooling systems modified so that some water being pumped by the fire pump was circulated through the truck's engine. This 1920 Mack AC had a 500 gpm pump and was used in New Brunswick, New Jersey. (Photo courtesy John J. Robrecht and Dick Adelman)

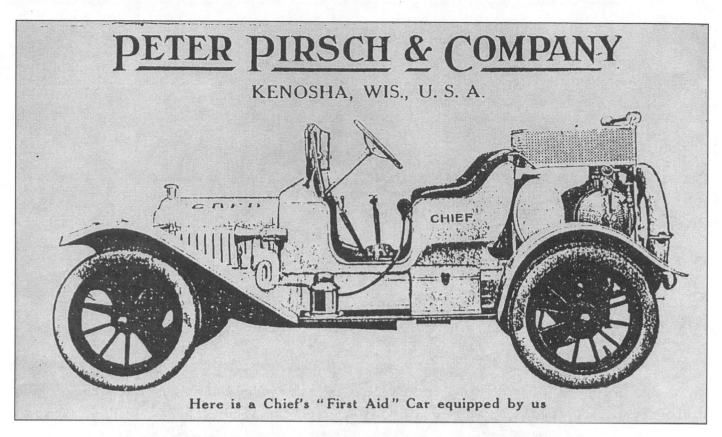

A Pirsch ad from about 1920 showing a "Chief's 'First Aid' Car" that they outfitted.

Working at a fire with its hood raised is Chicago's Engine 26, a 1920 Stutz model C with a Northern 750 gpm pump. The power plant was a Waukesha engine. The top half of the nearest headlight lens is red. (Photo courtesy Kenneth Little)

A circa-1920 White used as a Chicago city service truck. Near the front seat note the foot-operated gong and the hand-cranked siren. Between the head-lights a rolled-up cover is visible. When down, it covered the radiator to protect it from freezing spray. (Photo courtesy Volvo/White)

A 1920 Winther outfitted by Pirsch with a seventy-five-foot aerial lifted by a Dahill air hoist. The tiller is on the right side of the ladder. In 1929, Virginia, Minnesota (the truck's original owner) traded it in, and it was sold to St. Olaf's College in Northfield. At that later time the ladder lifting mechanism was converted to hydraulic power. (Photo courtesy Pirsch)

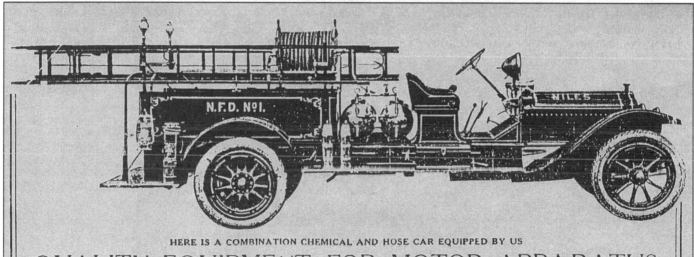

HERE IS A COMBINATION CHEMICAL AND HOSE CAR EQUIPPED BY US

QUALITY EQUIPMENT FOR MOTOR APPARATUS

LADDERS,   CHEMICAL TANKS,
BODIES, REELS   BASKETS, Etc.

WE MAKE THEM ALL, GET IN TOUCH WITH US BEFORE BUYING

WRITE FOR CATALOGUE

PETER PIRSCH & COMPANY

KENOSHA, WIS., U. S. A.

A Pirsch ad from about 1920 showing a White combination chemical and hose car for which they supplied the equipment.

Circa-1920 White fire boat tender number one, used in Cleveland, Ohio. Fire boat tenders responded to fire boat alarms and assisted from the landward side of the fire. (Photo courtesy Volvo/White)

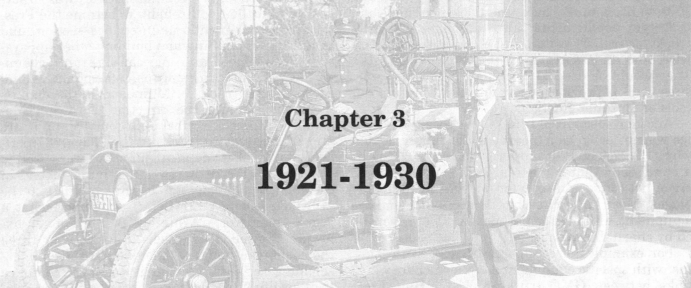

Chapter 3

1921-1930

*T*his would be the decade when autos and trucks swept the United States in terms of ownership and usage. In the fire apparatus field, makers of commercial trucks began selling specialized bodies on their trucks, including pumpers and ladder trucks (the latter usually mounted on school bus chassis). "Name" apparatus builders also turned out fine custom apparatus. In the very prosperous 1920s, communities did not hesitate to buy the best.

During this decade, horses would be retired completely from the fire service. In Detroit in 1922, Engine Company 37 was the last to give up use of horses, and the event was marked by a parade on Woodward Avenue. The last run was ceremonial, and the horses passed by a reviewing stand at Detroit's City Hall where "the Mayor, the Common Council, the Fire Commissioner, and retired officers of the Department were on hand to celebrate the event."[1]

Virtually all apparatus were painted red, and had one or more forward-facing fixed lights with red lenses. Bells were commonly used, as were hand-crank sirens. Electric sirens were coming into use, but the truck's lights would noticeably dim as the electric siren roared.

One new piece of equipment that came into use was known as the "quad," short for quadruple combination. Essentially, it combined the function of a pumper and a ladder truck. An American-LaFrance catalog of the era listed equipment for their Standard Type 14 Combination City Service Hook and Ladder Truck with a 600 gpm rotary pump, which included a hose rack capable of car-

rying 1000 feet of 2-1/2-inch hose, a 40-gallon chemical tank, and ladders consisting of a 50-foot and a 35-foot extension ladder, a 28-foot single ladder, two 25-foot single ladders, and four other smaller ladders for a total of 235 feet of ladder equipment. In this era, Chicago bought three Seagrave quads. Quads, however, had two disadvantages. At a major fire when both ladders and pumping capability were needed at the same time, the truck could be spotted either at the hydrant or at the burning structure. Secondly, usual-sized crews could not simultaneously handle pumping, hoses, and ladders. Quads sold well to suburbs that had volunteer firefighters and only a few tall buildings where long ladders might be needed.

Fireboats were also important. In the early 1920s the Marine Division of FDNY was operating eleven fireboats, with the largest having a pumping capability of 4500 gallons per minute. Land-based trucks often ran in conjunction with fireboats and helped lay hoses inland that could use the fireboat pumps' output. Not all fireboats were large. Some were small so that they could move under piers to fight fires.

Because of the widespread use of gasoline, there was an increased incidence of fires involving gasoline or other petroleum products. Water by itself could not be used to fight such fires; instead water-based foam solutions had to be employed. Some apparatus carried small foam hoppers and canisters of powder. Larger departments had one or more specialized foam trucks. In addition to having foam generating capability, the trucks carried long pipes that could be used to reach the

---

[1] *The American City* (August 1922), p. 138.

fire's edge. The trucks sometimes carried asbestos suits so firefighters could work closer to the heat.

Large departments also purchased "light" trucks or trailers containing a generator, coils of wire, and an assortment of movable floodlights. They would be used to illuminate fire or disaster sites and to provide power for operating rescue tools or for other emergency uses.

Another specialized type of truck was the "coffee wagon," such as appeared in Baltimore in the early 1920s. The Baltimore rig was a Ford T with a panel body that carried large thermos containers of hot coffee and soup for firefighters at major blazes. Most large cites had trucks with similar equipment, although sometimes they were operated by charitable groups.

For examples of commercial trucks with "tie-ins" with specific equipment suppliers, there were links between GMC trucks and the Hale Fire Pump Company of Conshohocken, Pennsylvania; and between International Trucks and Oberchain-Boyer, Buffalo, and Northern Fire Apparatus. FWD built a small number of apparatus with Waterous pumps. The Prospect Fire Engine Company of Prospect, Ohio, used Biederman chassis. The Buffalo Fire Appliance Corporation liked to use Larrabee chassis. Fire departments also purchased commercial chassis and outfitted them with specialized bodies. San Francisco bought some Klieber tractors for pulling city service (ladder) trailers, and other Kliebers were used to mount floodlights. San Francisco used a circa-1920 Kissel as a fuel wagon, carrying 500 gallons of gasoline and 100 gallons of oil (which indicates something about motor oil consumption in that era).

This was also the first of several decades when one hears or reads about "shop-built" apparatus. This has several meanings. For small communities it might mean buying a used truck chassis, say, a tank truck, and then ordering a pump and other equipment from a W. S. Darley catalog and having the equipment installed in a local blacksmith or machinist's shop. Paid departments also built some of their own equipment. In our *Volunteer . . .* book we show a 1930 Chevrolet city service truck that the on-duty paid firefighters in Fort Collins, Colorado, assembled using equipment supplied by W. S. Darley. Somewhat earlier, in Fresno, a Kissel chemical car was damaged in a fire and the firefighters agreed to repair and rebuild the damaged rig on their own time, using facilities made available by a neighboring

blacksmith shop. The rebuilding effort was so successful that the two firefighters became the Fresno Fire Department's maintenance section, and they began rebuilding and building other apparatus. This included an American-LaFrance chemical engine, some tank wagons, some pumpers, and a city service truck. In Minneapolis, the department shops under the direction of Master Mechanic William F. Stribel built fourteen pumpers and six city service trucks in the 1926-1931 period. In Milwaukee, department shops were used to convert two Pierce-Arrow autos into a chemical car and a squad wagon, respectively. In 1926 the Milwaukee shops built their first pumper, using a Waukesha motor, a Waterous pump, Timken axles, and Sewell disk wheels. Slightly over three thousand man-hours of labor were involved in assembling the pumper and it passed acceptance tests easily. The Milwaukee shops completed thirteen more pumpers in the period 1926-1931, usually using FWD chassis. The shops also built "boat wagons" (to accompany and work with fireboats) and three rescue squads.

Rescue squads ran with special equipment. Just after World War I, the Cincinnati Fire Department outfitted a rescue squad with the following equipment: one gas shut-off key; 100 feet of hoisting rope; two Barrett jacks; two hydraulic jacks; one leather bucket; three gallon extinguishers; one lift gun with rope; one portable telephone, two Lungmotors; nine helmets (including some with oxygen equipment); two leather pillows for Lungmotors; two wool blankets; one fifty-gallon chemical tank; 250 feet of one-inch hose; one Detroit door jamb; one carbide search light; three pairs of waterproof pants; two pairs of rubber gloves; one acetylene steel-cutting torch; one oxygen tank; one acetylene gas tank, and one hand ax.[2]

A few large cities used motorcycles that ran as part of "flying" squads, used to augment personnel at major fires. A firefighter riding the motorcycle (often with a partner in a sidecar) would race to the fire and could make better speed because of the cycle's maneuverability. The cycle would also be equipped with hand extinguishers.

During World War I, soldiers had been furnished with gas masks and, at the war's end, both large fire departments (and the U.S. Bureau of Mines) were interested in peacetime use of the masks. Testing showed that conventional military masks would be of limited use at most fires, since they filtered only very specific gases. Oxygen-sup-

---

[2] *The American City* (December 1922), p. 525.

plying masks would be more useful, but for many years only a few rescue squads would be supplied with them.

This was also the decade when chain drive would be phased out, although some manufacturers would offer chain drive into the mid-1930s. One reason it would last was that it was cheaper than worm drive, which may have been important in the municipal bidding process. (Chain drive did require more care and maintenance—which the bidding process often overlooked.) In 1920 Ahrens-Fox introduced its Model J, which was chainless and available on either hard-rubber or pneumatic tires. Ahrens-Fox delivered its last chain drive units in 1923. They began building city service trucks with two banks of ladders, side by side, which lowered the truck's center of gravity. They also built aerial ladder trucks, incorporating the Dahill Air Hoist. In the late 1920s, Ahrens-Fox began building midship-mounted rotary pumpers. For Ahrens-Fox, the 1920s would be its best years. In appearance, nothing could beat its front-mount pump with a polished globe. On the dash was mounted a Van Deusen bell with the engraved instructions: "Every few months turn bell slightly so clapper will not always strike in same place." Sales were good with deliveries made to most major U.S. cities such as Akron, Atlantic City, Baltimore, Buffalo, Chicago, Cincinnati, Detroit, Kansas City, Missouri, Long Beach, Los Angeles, Louisville, New Orleans, New York City, Newark, Passaic, Paterson, San Francisco, Seattle, St. Louis, St. Paul, and Tulsa.

The 1920s were also good to American-LaFrance, which introduced its Type 12 rotary pumper in 1921, available with either chain or shaft drive. In a 1926 statement, the firm said that in the period from 1910 until 1926, they had sold over four thousand rotary gear pumpers, forty-one piston pumpers, and five centrifugal pumpers. A new model was introduced, called the "100 series." From this time forward, subsequent models were named "200 series," "300 series," and so on. In 1927 the firm acquired the Foamite Childs Corporation, and the new firm was known as the American-LaFrance and Foamite Corporation. The "200 series" was introduced in 1929 and featured left-hand steering and all-wheel brakes. The pumpers had an improved cooling capability that allowed water the pumper was pumping to circulate through the engine using different plumbing than the radiator's conventional cooling system (which might also contain anti-freeze). In 1937 Louisville received an American-LaFrance quad that had bench seating for firefighters, with seats on each side of the truck, parallel to the truck. This was an early move in making the ride to the fire safer for the firefighters. Major U.S. cities that bought American-LaFrance equipment in the 1920s included Albany; Baltimore; Boston; Camden; Indianapolis; Los Angeles; Memphis; Minneapolis; New York; Oakland, California; Philadelphia; Pittsburgh; Pocatello; Reading; Rochester; San Francisco; Seattle; and Syracuse.

Buffalo supplied Ford truck dealers and Stewart truck dealers with fully equipped apparatus on the dealers' make of chassis.

In San Jose, California, FMC began selling John Bean high pressure fog systems, which made use of limited amounts of water, an advantage in rural areas. In addition, after the fire was extinguished, there was less water damage to the structure, an advantage of the units in urban areas. FMC units were mounted and sold on commercial chassis.

In 1923 the Foamite Firefoam Company and O. J. Childs merged to form the Foamite Childs Corporation. They began building chemical cars and pumpers, and in the late 1920s introduced their custom chassis, known as "Child's Thoroughbreds."

General Manufacturing Company in St. Louis built fire extinguishers, and in the mid-1920s began building motorized apparatus on commercial chassis. In 1926 the firm's name was changed to the General Fire Truck Corporation. For a brief time they had a close association with Studebaker, mounting their apparatus on Studebaker and Pierce-Arrow chassis (Pierce-Arrow was owned by Studebaker at this time). In the late 1920s, the firm produced a custom model called the "General Monarch," which had its pump controls in the cowl.

Mack was probably the best-known make of medium and large trucks during the 1920s. The AC "Bulldogs" were especially popular. At the end of World War I, Baltimore purchased a number of war-surplus Mack ACs and built them into pumpers, high pressure hose wagons, city service trucks, and tractors for pulling aerial ladders. They also had a department wrecker installed on an AC chassis. In the late 1920s, Mack introduced an AL model, which looked like a lowered, streamlined version of the Bulldog, and was initially intended for intercity bus use. Some fire apparatus were built on AL chassis. Mack marketed its own line of apparatus and Mack chassis were also used by other apparatus outfitters. San Francisco's first apparatus with four-wheel brakes were two Mack pumpers delivered in 1927. They had 1000 gpm Byron-Jackson parallel-series centrifugal pumps.

Northern Fire Apparatus Company of Minneapolis was best-known as a builder and supplier of pumps. It also outfitted apparatus on commercial chassis. Its name appeared in ads as a pump supplier for various makes of apparatus. For a while, it marketed a trailer-mounted pump that was to be pulled by motorized hose wagons.

Pirsch started the 1920s building apparatus on chassis supplied by others, including several large orders of hose wagons mounted on International and on FWD chassis. In 1926 Pirsch began building custom units powered by Waukesha motors. A "first" sometimes credited to Pirsch was an enclosed cab on a custom unit, delivered in 1928.

Sanford trucks were built in Syracuse, and their chassis were often used by Oberchain-Boyer and Foamite Childs to complete apparatus. In 1925 Sanford began building its own apparatus using Waterous rotary gear pumps. In turn, they began outfitting commercial chassis built by others, including Ford.

Seagrave introduced its round-hood model in 1921, which would stay in production until 1935. Seagrave received a big order from Chicago in the early 1920s for 39 model F-76 750 gpm centrifugal pumpers. They had a hand lever between the driver's seat and the officer's seat to activate the flywheel-mounted siren. In Chicago the apparatus had red and green lenses, apparently relying on street lights for night-time illumination. There was a bench set over the hose box. There was a bell tower in front of the radiator and soft suction hose was carried on the right running board. They ran on pneumatic tires. Later in the decade, Chicago ordered five more pumpers, five eighty-five-foot tractor-drawn aerials, and two quads from Seagrave. Los Angeles was an even better customer of Seagrave, ordering sixty-six pieces of apparatus during the 1920s. Seagrave's ladder trucks continued to rely on spring-raised aerials. In 1923 Seagrave introduced its "suburbanite" model intended for sale to suburban communities. The model would also be used as hose wagons in New York City.

The 1920s were not very kind to Stutz. In 1919 the firm's pumper had outshone all rivals at a fire chiefs' convention, and sales boomed. However, in 1926 a dispute over management and financial control resulted in the collapse of the firm. In the early '20s it had done well, selling about three hundred pieces of apparatus, mainly its famous pumper. U.S. cities using Stutz apparatus included Baltimore; Boise; Chicago; Davenport; Denver; Duluth; Gary; Indianapolis (a 1921 Stutz ad proclaimed: "25 pumpers and 10 [city] service trucks in daily service in Indianapolis"); Kansas City, Kansas; Lima; Los Angeles; Portland, Oregon; San Francisco; San Jose; Spokane; St. Louis; Suffolk, Virginia; Washington, D.C.; and Wichita Falls. In late 1929 H. C. Mecklenburg, who had been a principal in the earlier Stutz firm, opened a new firm and had permission to use the Stutz name. The intent of the new firm was to service existing Stutz apparatus, and to build new apparatus.

In 1927 in northern California, F. E. Van Pelt began building water tankers with small pumps for use by rural fire departments. One of the reasons for the success of his product was that he used hot rivets for the tanks and they held better than cold rivets, which would pop out on rough roads.

New York's fire department always bought in large quantities. In 1921 they purchased twenty American-LaFrance pumpers, ten aerials pulled by Macks, ten White/Pirsch combination chemical city service trucks, a rescue wagon, and a fireboat. By the end of 1921, all of FDNY's ladder units were motorized. In 1922 a fuel tender to carry gasoline was delivered, mounted on a FWD chassis. By 1925 FDNY was completely motorized, and its remaining horses were sold. In 1927 they purchased an Ahrens-Fox pumper that had the distinction of being their first rig with pneumatic tires. In 1929 and 1930 a batch of Walter tractors was received.

As for salvage corps equipment, in Albany a 1923 custom Seagrave was purchased. Baltimore's corps bought a 1927 Mack, adding a renovated body, and in 1928 a Ford T was purchased that had a Barton front-mount pump used for pumping out basements. Boston added some Macks, with bodies by Abbot & Downing. Chicago's corps began buying Yellow Coach trucks (made by GM), and Diamond-Ts. San Francisco's patrol bought two REOS. General Fire Truck Corporation of St. Louis outfitted a 1927 REO for that city's salvage corps to utilize. During this decade, the Worcester Protective Department bought a 1921 GMC and a 1924 Ahrens-Fox.

During the 1920s, there was considerable development into suburbs, and many new fire stations were built. Many were one-story high, keeping in character of neighborhoods where they were placed. Firemen would sleep in ground-floor rooms and run to board the apparatus, rather than sliding down brass poles. Most stations still needed hose-drying towers, approximately thirty feet high, but a few built drying racks that had hose resting at an angle. Some cities built large new headquarters buildings downtown. Detroit opened their new five-story building in 1925. At the corner of Larned Street and Wayne Street, the building had a frontage of about 120 feet on each. In the basement was a garage that could hold thirty autos, with spaces used by chiefs and visiting officials. On the main floor was an apparatus room with three exits on one street and four on the other. It housed three chiefs' cars, a high-pressure apparatus, a water tower, a ladder truck, an engine, and an ambulance. There were seven slide poles for the men and one for the chief. On the first floor were the kitchen, the dining room, a lounge area, entrance to the hose tower, and signal boards for receiving alarms. On the second floor were sleeping accommodations for forty men, plus rooms for the officers. On the third and fourth floors were offices for the chiefs, the fire commission, the fire prevention bureau, a physician, etc. The fifth floor was unoccupied and available for expansion.[3]

During the entire decade, communities, at the urging of the National Board of Fire Underwriters, standardized hydrant and hose couplings and fittings. This was an important step because it allowed apparatus from distant communities to be called in to assist during major blazes. Eventually, nearly every department in the nation would be part of mutual aid agreements, meaning that they would back each other up when needed. In 1928 the fire chief of Charlotte, North Carolina, announced that a mutual aid pact had been entered into with nine other communities: Chester, Concord, Gastonia, Lincolnton, Monroe, Mooresville, Rock Hill, Salisbury, and Statesville. He noted that roads between the communities were "paved" and that "the fire-fighting apparatus of all towns will be standardized and all engine pumpers and hose can be connected with any hydrant in the system."[4]

This was also the decade in which departments in many cities began programs of regular fire inspections. The purpose of the inspections was to eliminate, or at least reduce, the number of potentially hazardous practices and conditions inside buildings.

At the decade's end, Ralph J. Scott, chief of the Los Angeles Fire Department and president of the International Association of Fire Chiefs, wrote an article summarizing two decades of developments in the fire fighting profession. The improvements he cited were:

1. Abolishing the 24-hour system and replacing it with the two-platoon system.
2. Improvement in pension systems for professional firefighters.
3. Improvement in firefighters' wages, compared with other callings.
4. Technical training for firefighters.
5. Salvage work with the goal being to reduce damage to a structure's contents as the fire is being fought.
6. Rescue work becoming a recognized responsibility of fire departments.
7. Motorization of apparatus.
8. Fire prevention activities.
9. Adoption of building and electrical codes.[5]

[3] *The American City* (October 1929), p. 147.

[4] *The American City* (August 1928), p. 146.

[5] Ralph J. Scott, "Twenty-One Years of Progress in Fighting and Preventing Fires," *The American City* (September 1930), pp. 108-110.

Ford Motor Company of Canada used this Ford AA, outfitted by Bickle, for plant protection. It carried several chemical tanks.

This 1920s photo shows two Chicago fire engines working off a dual hydrant. In the foreground is Engine 7, a 1921 Ahrens-Fox model I M 2 with a 750 gpm pump.

Boston ran this huge, circa-1921 American-LaFrance high pressure hose wagon as High Pressure No. 3. It had two large turret pipes and a chemical tank, with chemical hose carried in a basket. On the far side behind the seat is a Whiting warning light. (Photo courtesy Charles E. Beckwith)

In 1920 Indianapolis ordered thirty-five pieces of apparatus from the Stutz Fire Engine Company, located in the same city. Shown here is one of the engines, a 1921 Stutz model B with a 600 gpm pump. It ran as Engine 10. Note the pre-connected suction hose. (Photo courtesy Charles A. Waugaman)

This is a 1921 Stutz Model B 600 gpm triple combination pumper used by Indianapolis. In service as Hose 23. (Photo courtesy Dan G. Martin)

A 1921 Traylor chassis built by the Traylor Engineering and Manufacturing Company of Allentown, used by the Philadelphia Fire Department to mount a chemical and hose body that had originally been on a 1912 Boyd. (Photo courtesy Gus Johnson)

Detroit used this 1922 Ahrens-Fox Model J-13 high pressure hose wagon with two large Morse turret pipes. The hose box carried three-inch hose for supplying the turrets. (Photo courtesy Dan Martin)

In the early 1920s, Chicago purchased thirty-three Ahrens-Fox 750 gpm pumpers. Twenty years later it was impossible to receive new apparatus because of World War II, so the Chicago Fire Department shops had to forge large crankshafts to keep some of the venerable Ahrens-Fox rigs running. Shown here is Engine 107, originally built in 1921. In 1951 the shops installed a Cummins diesel engine. (Photo courtesy Dick Adelman and Stanley Helberg)

Philadelphia's Bureau of Fire used this 1922 five-ton Mack AC as a wrecker. It served until 1948. (Photo courtesy Wayne Sorensen Collection)

Winona, Minnesota, used this early '20s Oshkosh four-wheel drive tractor to pull its aerial ladder. The ladder was raised quickly by compressed springs. The two-handled crank was used to lower the ladder. The crank beyond the lantern was for extending the ladder once it was elevated. The truck also carried a variety of ground ladders. On the trailer a number of braces and struts are visible. (Photo courtesy Oshkosh Truck Corporation)

Los Angeles Engine 2, an early 1920s Stutz, after a fender-bender. (Photo courtesy Blackhawk Classic Auto Collection)

Engine 4 in Somerville, Massachusetts, used this 1922 Seagrave 1300 gpm pumper. Note the shield to protect the hose from being cut on the runningboard. (Photo courtesy Gus Johnson)

Denver used this 1922 Model O Stutz as Engine 6. The 1000 gpm pumper is shown supplying two hose lines. Power was provided by a Wisconsin six-cylinder Type M engine.

Again Stutz Wins

Lawrence, Mass., buys seven pieces Stutz Apparatus after thorough consideration of all makes

QUALITY fire apparatus—thoroughly dependable equipment big and powerful enough to meet any possible emergency—was what the Lawrence officials wanted.

In deciding on the seven Stutz—four 750 gal. triple combinations and three city service trucks—they satisfied themselves that the city was getting real up-to-the-minute fire apparatus and the best money could buy.

*Ask us tell you more about Stutz apparatus—
to show you why it is best suited to your needs*

STUTZ FIRE ENGINE COMPANY

INDIANAPOLIS **INDIANA**

This Stutz ad appeared in Fire and Water Engineering in 1922.

In 1923 San Francisco's Fire Department assembled representative apparatus in front of city hall. In the front center is a circa-1923 open Stutz auto, the chief's buggy. Looking at the next full row, we see, from left to right, a 1914 American-LaFrance front-drive tractor attached to a 1914 Metropolitan 2nd size, 700 gpm steam pumper; a circa-1918 Seagrave 750 gpm pumper; a circa-1915 American-LaFrance high pressure battery wagon with a Gorter turret; a 1914 American-LaFrance squad wagon; and a 1917 American-LaFrance chemical engine. In the next row are a 1915 Schneer combination chemical and hose wagon, a circa-1915 Seagrave city service truck, a 1921 American-LaFrance tractor attached to a 1902 Gorter seventy-five-foot water tower, and a 1923 Buick coffee wagon. The most distant rig is a circa-1918 Seagrave 750 gpm pumper. (Photo courtesy San Francisco Fire Department)

Mission, Texas, purchased this 1923 American-LaFrance Type 40 triple combination. It carried a 350 gpm gear pump, a forty-gallon chemical tank with 200 feet of 3/4-inch hose, 1200 feet of 2-1/2-inch hose, two ladders, several lanterns, and extinguishers. The siren is operated by a hand crank. (Photo courtesy American-LaFrance)

This is one of three 1923 American-LaFrance, Type 56, 750 gpm piston pumpers purchased by Baltimore. Note the fourteen-inch, sixty-pound Dietz-Romer bell and the Holloway chemical tank. The engine also had an exhaust-heated, hydrant-thawing device. (Photo courtesy American-LaFrance)

Baltimore operated a fleet of Ahrens-Fox apparatus. Shown is a 1923 model KS3 with a 750 gpm pump. At the time of this photo it was serving as second line Engine 23 (in reserve). (Photo courtesy John J. Robrecht)

FDNY's Water Tower Number 2 is shown at the left, working at a warehouse fire. The sixty-five-foot tower is a 1904 Femco/Hale, pulled by a 1923 Mack AC-6. In the foreground is an aerial ladder pulled by a Mack AC-7. (Photo courtesy Gus A. Johnson)

The City of Los Angeles outfitted four foam trucks on 1923 Moreland chassis to fight oil well fires. Foam powder was carried in five-gallon cans in the truck's bed. The powder was placed in a hopper known as a foam generator (see funnel resting upside down on running board) and added to a stream of water. Pipes or overshoots were carried to allow foam to be placed at the base of fires. The Moreland trucks were built in Burbank and the one shown here was powered by a 32 hp four-cylinder Hercules engine. (Photo courtesy Dale Magee)

In 1923 Maxim Motor Company introduced a "new look" with a gabled hood and massive radiator. The triple combination pump is mounted below the seat. (Photo courtesy Maxim)

This 1923 Bulldog Mack, with a C cab, was used by the Philadelphia Fire Department to carry fuel. It was in service until the end of World War II. (Photo courtesy John J. Robrecht)

WILLIAMANTIC, CONN.

Williamantic, Connecticut, used this circa-1923 Mack AC to pull its tillered aerial. (Photo courtesy Dick Adelman)

This pumper, with bodywork by Pirsch, was mounted on a 1923 Stoughton body. It's shown at an auction in 1988.

A close-up view of a Stutz Model O, 1200 gpm rotary-gear pumper at work in Roseburg, Oregon in 1924. The hood is up for cooling the Wisconsin engine. (Photo courtesy Douglas County Museum)

West New York, New Jersey's Engine 4 was a 1924, 1000 gpm American-LaFrance that had been modernized with a new radiator, hood, cowl, and fuel tank. (Photo courtesy John J. Robrecht)

Engine No. 6 in Lynn, Massachusetts, was a 750 gpm Ahrens-Fox, shown covered with ice. (Photo courtesy Don Young)

A CT Electric from the 1920s outfitted to work in New York's Holland Tunnel as a wrecker and recovery truck. It was also equipped to fight gasoline fires in the tunnel. (Photo courtesy Port Authority of New York and New Jersey)

In the early 1920s, Ford Model T cars and Model TT trucks were the most popular make in the U.S. Many were used in the fire service. In large cities they served as hose wagons and as departmental service trucks. They were the backbone of many suburban and rural fire departments. This picture shows the first Barton front-mount pump on a 1924 Ford TT. The customer was Mitchfield, Michigan. (Photo courtesy Dick Adelman)

A 1924 GMC hose and chemical car used as Chemical 8 in San Jose. (Photo courtesy Wayne Sorensen)

Washington. D.C.'s Truck 3 was a 1924 Seagrave model L856, with an eighty-five-foot spring-raised aerial. Note steel disk wheels and solid tires. (Photo courtesy Seagrave)

A mid-20s American-LaFrance tractor pulling a thirty-two-foot deluge tower for Engine 1 in Pittsburgh. The truck also carried two deck guns and 1000 feet of 2-1/2-inch hose. (Photo courtesy American-LaFrance)

Foamite Childs Corporation of Utica supplied the foam units for this 1925 American LaFrance chemical car, which ran as Boston's Foamite 1. It carried four sixty-gallon chemical tanks and two hose reels. (Photo courtesy Dick Adelman)

This is one of two American-LaFrance Type 17 eighty-five-foot aerial ladders purchased by FDNY in 1925. Note the leather wind protector above the cowl. Power was provided by a 105 hp, 6-cylinder motor. (Photo courtesy Gus Johnson)

A 1925 Ford TT used by the Baltimore Salvage Corps as Wagon No. 8. The front-mount pump was used for pumping out flooded basements. (Photo courtesy Wayne Sorensen Collection)

An insurance patrol truck used in Chicago. Chassis is a 1924 White, model 51. Hose bed area has crew seats and storage for tarpaulins. (Photo courtesy Volvo/White)

Parades are important to fire departments in a public relations sense, and fire engines and trucks are a regular ingredient in most community parades. Bedecked with flags and ready to parade is Allenhurst, New Jersey's 1925 Stutz Model HR 600 gpm quad. (Photo courtesy Bill Schwartz)

Atlantic City bought this 1926 American-LaFrance eighty-five-foot aerial ladder to run as Truck 3. The tractor is a restyled 100 Series with a high radiator and a recessed cowl. (Photo courtesy John J. Robrecht)

Boston's 1893 Hale fifty-five-foot water tower being towed by a 1926 American-LaFrance Type 17 tractor. Later, a tiller steering device was installed on the trailer. (Photo courtesy Gus Johnson)

In 1926 the Kleiber Motor Company of San Francisco built two truck-tractors to pull city service trailers for that city's fire department. In 1928 they were reassigned to pull 1902 vintage Gorter water towers. This photo was taken in 1976. (Photo courtesy Wayne Sorensen)

A 1926 Mack AB Series triple combination pumper with worm drive. The radiator type is referred to as "high hat." A chemical tank is behind the seat. The rotary gear pump was built by Northern. (Photo courtesy Mack)

A 1926 Mack Model AB used as a high pressure hose car unit in Albany. It has a turret gun, and the gun's inlets are visible. Hose units usually ran as half of a two-piece company, the other piece being a pumper.

The hood on this 1926 Mack AC is up, working at a fire. It has a 600 gpm Hale pump. The unit is Baltimore's SLE (Second Line Engine) 19, after renovation in the department's shops. The pumper served in first-line service from 1926 until 1947, and in reserve status from then until 1965.

Pierce-Arrow was best known for its autos, but it also built a high-quality truck. In 1926 FDNY purchased four Pierce-Arrow city service trucks that had been built by the Combination Ladder Company of New York City. This one was Ladder No. 76.

This rig is built on a 1926 Pierce-Arrow "Z" chassis, initially intended for buses. General outfitted the 500 gpm pumper for Fairview, New Jersey. It is shown here after being converted to a light truck.

Montgomery, Indiana, ran this 1926 Pirsch model 19 triple combination 500 gpm custom pumper. It carried twin chemical tanks. (Photo courtesy Pirsch and Dick Adelman)

Washington, D.C., used this 1926 Seagrave as Engine 9. On the hood is a picture of George Washington (a firefighter himself). Note gold trim on wheels. (Photo courtesy Seagrave)

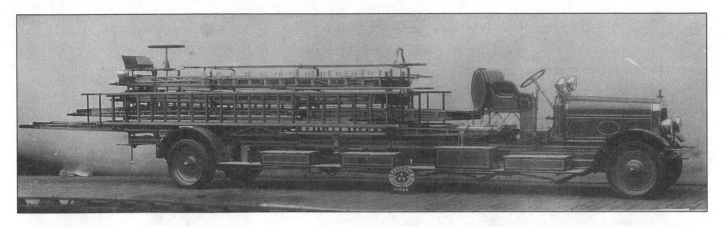

This solid-frame, tillered 1926 Seagrave city service truck was built for Los Angeles. It had right-hand steering, disc wheels, and solid tires. (Photo courtesy Seagrave)

This isn't a fire truck, but it's very closely related. It's a light truck used for night filming of a moving picture entitled *The Fire Brigade*. This truck was built to race alongside regular fire trucks in Los Angeles as they raced to a fire, and illuminate them so they could be photographed. A 1926 White Model 50-B bus chassis was used to carry the generator, lights, and cameramen. The MGM film was intended to "teach American cities the wisdom of keeping fire departments out of political entanglements and of having experienced firemen inspect all new building work," according to a White press release accompanying the original photo. (Photo courtesy Volvo/White)

A 1926 Seagrave combination chemical and hose car built for Brockton, Massachusetts. It has a flared hose body. The chemical tank is below the seat and the chemical hose is carried in the basket above the hose bed. (Photo courtesy Seagrave and FWD)

A circa-1927 American-LaFrance, Type 119, with a 1200 gpm Duplex High Pressure Pump. It ran as Engine 32 in Pittsburgh. (Photo courtesy American-LaFrance)

In 1927 American-LaFrance introduced its Metropolitan, Type 100 Series. This one went to the Rainbow Fire Company No. 1 of Reading, Pennsylvania. Later, new wheels and four-wheel brakes were installed. (Photo courtesy John J. Robrecht)

The business end of a 1927 Ahrens-Fox Model J52, Detroit's Engine 20. (Photo courtesy Wayne Sorensen Collection)

A 1927 Fageol auxiliary fire truck operated by the Market Street Railway (a streetcar system) in San Francisco. It was designed to be able to lift streetcars off of whatever or whoever was unfortunate enough to be under them. (Photo courtesy John Graham)

Kennett Square, Pennsylvania, had this 1927 Hale. Under the closest headlight, note the front suction hose inlet, unusual in that era. (Photo courtesy Carl Fridley)

A 1927 Hahn pumper with a Northern rotary pump used by the Audubon Park Fire Department. The pump had an automatic relief valve that enabled pipemen to shut off a nozzle without danger of bursting the hose or harming the pump. Note additional floodlights.

Chicago's Hook and Ladder Company 35 used this 1927 Mack AC tractor to pull its 1905 Seagrave eighty-five-foot wooden aerial. The half circle behind the side-mounted ladder is a life net. (Photo courtesy Dick Adelman)

San Francisco's Fire Department used this 1927 Mack AC chassis to carry a thirty-five-foot Gorter water tower installed by the Union Iron Works of San Francisco. A water-powered motor can be seen in front of the tower base; it was used to raise the tower. The tower has eight three-inch hose inlets, four on each side. (Photo courtesy Wayne Sorensen)

Chicago's Fire Department shops used a 1927 White 45 chassis to build High Pressure Hose No. 5. Armament includes the large-capacity turret pipes. The inlets are above running board level. (Photo courtesy Dick Adelman)

This is Philadelphia's 1928 American-LaFrance Type 119, 1250 gpm high pressure engine. It ran as Engine 20. Note chain drive and multisection hood louvres. (Photo courtesy John J. Robrecht)

Washington, D.C.'s Engine Company No. 4 was then called a "colored" company. Their engine was this 1928 American-LaFrance, Series 153, 750 gpm triple combination with hard tires and disk wheels. (Photo courtesy "Smoke House" Hardy)

Chicago's Engine 128, a 1928 Ahrens-Fox Model N-S-2, was one of seven purchased. (Photo courtesy Stanley Helberg)

Beverly Hills, California, purchased two of these 1928 Ahrens-Fox Model GN-80-4 rotary gear, 750 gpm pumpers. (Photo courtesy Dale Magee)

A 1928 Buffalo 500 gpm pumper purchased by the U.S. Army. It has a Kearns-Dughie chassis. The pump is below the seat, and behind the pump is a chemical tank. (Photo courtesy Buffalo Fire Appliance Company)

Chicago used a 1928 Ford AA to build this chemical rig. On the rear step is a carbon dioxide tank and on top of the bed is a foam hopper. (Photo courtesy Dick Adelman)

In 1928 FDNY bought nineteen hose wagons outfitted by Pirsch on FWD chassis. They carried large deck pipes and scaling ladders. Here we see Engine 263's wagon at a fire. (Photo courtesy Frank J. Fenning)

A 1928 International Series S with an ambulance body used by the Chicago Fire Department. (Photo courtesy Navistar Archives)

San Francisco used two 1928 Kleibers for light wagons. (Photo courtesy Paul Darrell)

Here is a 1928 Mack AL chassis, initially intended for intercity bus bodies, but used to carry a heavy city service body. The rig was used for Humane Company No. 1 in Rogerford, Pennsylvania. (Photo courtesy Roland Boulet)

This 1928 Pirsch 750 gpm pumper went to Monroe, Wisconsin. It is believed to be the first custom apparatus with an enclosed cab. Pirsch used Stoughton chassis at this time. (Photo courtesy Walt Schyver)

Milwaukee had a proud Socialist tradition and believed that a properly-run government could provide many services at lower cost than could private enterprise. For a while the city relied upon its shops to build apparatus. This 750 gpm pumper was designed and assembled in its shops, on a 1928 FWD chassis. Grille emblem says "M.F.D." (Photo courtesy Dick Adelman)

A 1928 Mack AC 7-1/2-ton chassis outfitted to fight oil fires, or for use where excessive water damage was to be avoided. It was used in Baltimore. It carried two 1000-gallon tanks, a small pump, and 300 feet of 3/4-inch hose on a reel. It was in service only for a short time.

Coral Gables, Florida, ran this late '20s REO chemical and hose unit. Between the headlights is the well-known REO spiderweb grille, protecting the radiator. (Photo courtesy Florida State Archives)

The Fresno Fire Department shops used a circa-1928 REO chassis to build a water wagon with a PTO-driven pump. It was assigned as Chemical 1. (Photo courtesy Laval Company, Inc.)

This is a 1928 Studebaker/Maxim used in Eastport, Maine. The 500 gpm pumper also carried ladders and chemical tanks. (Photo courtesy Dale Magee)

Los Angeles ran this 1928 Studebaker ambulance as Rescue No. 1, in service with Engine 23. Its equipment is displayed in front. (Photo courtesy Dick Adelman)

These two pictures help show the difference between two types of apparatus. Both are of 100 Series American-LaFrance purchased by Atlantic City, New Jersey, in the late 1920s. The top photo is of Engine 6, a 1928 1000 gpm pumper; the bottom is a 1929 combination hose and chemical car, which ran with Engine 8. Comparing the two, the main difference is that below the seat, one carries a pump, the other, one of several chemical tanks. The fenders are more streamlined on the 1929 models; apparatus builders were conscious of styling. (Photos courtesy John J. Robretch and Dick Adelman)

Cheviot, Ohio, bought a lot of fire truck when they ordered the first quad built by Ahrens-Fox, this 1929 model UM4 with a 750 gpm pump. The hose box is above the ladder rack, and at the top right we see the chute through which it is played out. A booster tank is behind the gas tank. (Photo courtesy Ahrens-Fox)

In 1929 Detroit purchased three Mack Type 19, 750 gpm pumpers. This one served as Engine 10 until 1952, when it was sold to the Franklin, Michigan, volunteer fire department. Note winter windbreaker. Headlights are not original. (Photo courtesy Dick Adelman)

In 1929 Seagrave delivered to FDNY a sixty-five-foot Hale water tower that was hydraulically raised. It had two nozzles on the mast. It was FDNY's first water tower with a tiller, although the tiller was intended for use only at the fire scene when the tower was being driven where there was considerable hose and parked apparatus in the area. When traveling to and from stations, the tiller wheel was locked. It had sixteen inlets. In 1957 this and FDNY's other towers were retired. The tractor was one of Seagrave's last with right-hand steering, chain drive, and hard tires. (Photo courtesy J. J. Lerch and Dick Adelman)

This is one of five Seagrave combination hose and chemical cars that Los Angeles purchased in 1929. Note spare tire. The red light is on the right side of the cowl (on most apparatus it was on the left, to be better seen by oncoming traffic). (Photo courtesy Seagrave)

This 1929 Sanford has a Waterous 600 gpm rotary gear pump and booster equipment. White sidewalls are unusual, as is the windshield, which looks like a canvas one was fitted to cover the gap below the fixed one. This pumper was used in Towaco, New Jersey. (Photo courtesy Dick Adelman)

Note the red headlight lenses on Chicago's Ladder 49 1929 White model 59 tractor. It is pulling a 1922 Seagrave eighty-five-foot aerial ladder. (Photo courtesy Volvo/White)

Memphis used this 1930 American-LaFrance Series 200, 1000 gpm pumper for training purposes after it was retired from first-line service. The windshield, top, and sealed-beam headlights had been added by that department's shops. (Photo courtesy Dick Adelman)

The Underwriters Salvage Corps of Cincinnati purchased this 1930 Ahrens-Fox salvage car mounted on a LeBlond-Schacht chassis. It had a V-12 engine. (Photo courtesy Ahrens-Fox)

A circa-1930 Buffalo custom Type 100 C-1, 1000 gpm, rotary gear, triple combination pumper in service as Engine 12 in Lynn, Massachusetts. This is one of five Buffalos that Lynn would purchase. (Photo courtesy Bob Fitz and Dick Adelman)

The San Francisco Fire Department had a high pressure water hydrant system that relied on reservoirs located in the city's hills. When high pressure was needed to combat a blaze, certain valves and gates had to be opened to direct the water into large-diameter pipes that supplied a series of large-diameter, high-pressure hydrants. Two trucks like this were employed. They carried a hydraulic spindle that could reach to either side, used to open and close the valves that were accessed through small covers in the street. The truck is a 1930 Ford AA. (Photo courtesy Wayne Sorensen)

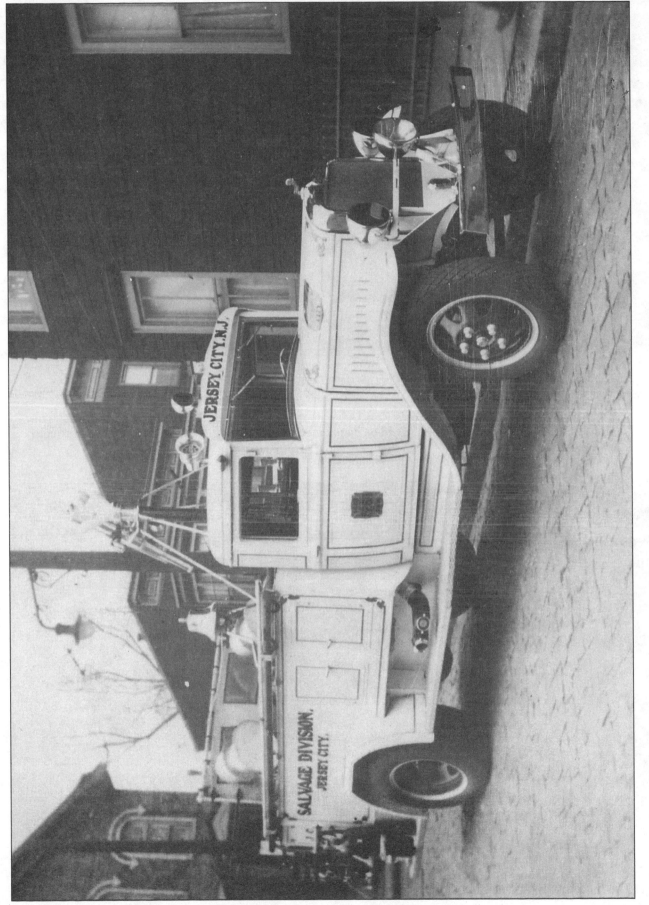

Salvage 26 in Jersey City was built on a 1930 GMC chassis. It carries a mounted turret, floodlights, and a windshield to protect those riding on the rear step.

This is a 1930 GMC light truck operated by Boston's Fire Department. These types of vehicles fall into a category sometimes referred to as "special call" trucks: they would be dispatched only in response to a specific call. (Photo courtesy Charles E. Beckwith)

A 1930 International (or Fishcher) pulling a city service trailer that has no tiller. In service as Truck 2 in Fort Williams, Ontario. (Photo courtesy Wayne Sorensen Collection)

This 1930 Mack B Series open-cab tractor was used by Trenton, New Jersey, to pull a 1916 Boyd seventy-five-foot aerial ladder for Truck 3. Mudflaps have been added behind all the wheels. (Photo courtesy John J. Robrecht)

FDNY Engine 244's 1930 Mack 700 gpm pumper at a Coney Island fire in 1940. Note the tarps covering the front of the rig and the hose line supplying the turret. At left note the "subway straps" at the rear of the other fire engine. (Photo courtesy Lynn Sams)

One of seven 1930 Mack AC Bulldogs purchased by FDNY. Windshield and pneumatic tires were added later. This unit was first assigned to Engine 267, and was later assigned to Engine 341 as a spare. (Photo courtesy Frank J. Fenning)

Checking alignment on a 1930 Pirsch 500 gpm pumper.

Kenosha, Wisconsin, home of Pirsch, used this 1930 Pirsch city service truck with a chemical tank. A bell is mounted in front of the radiator. Note the seven-man crew. (Photo courtesy Pirsch and Dick Adelman)

Jersey City operated this 1930 REO that carried two high-pressure turrets. The truck is painted white with red lenses in the headlights. The door on the cab slides. (Photo courtesy Charles E. Beckwith)

This is FDNY's Hose Wagon 6, mounted on a 1930 Seagrave "Suburbanite" chassis. Inlets are for a deck gun. This was one of an order of twenty-three. (Photo courtesy Dick Adelman)

Teaneck, New Jersey, bought a 1930 Model 65K White tractor to replace a 1921 Mack AC for pulling a 1921 seventy-five-foot aerial that had originally been purchased by FDNY.

In 1930 FDNY purchased six Walter tractors. This one was used to pull Tower 5, a 1907 spring-raised Seagrave sixty-five-foot tower. At the rear of the trailer is a deck-level turret. (Photo courtesy John J. Robrecht)

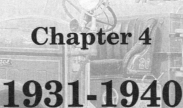

Chapter 4
1931-1940

*T*his was the decade of the "Great Depression." Professional firefighters felt lucky to have regular paying jobs. Movie news reels showed large fires. New York City's colorful mayor, Fiorello H. La Guardia, was a fire buff and would be at the scene of any large fire in his city.

The spirit of professionalism continued and time was devoted to training. A course for firefighters sponsored by the New York State Fire Chiefs' Association covered the following subjects: auxiliary equipment, building inspection, care of equipment, courtesy, exposures, fighting different types of fires, fire prevention, first aid, forcible entry, hydraulics, operation of equipment, salvage, and ventilation. The Fire Chiefs' Association also recommended that each department construct and maintain its own training tower, saying: "An appropriation for a training tower is one of the best investments a municipality can make. It will more than pay for itself in fire-fighting efficiency the first year."[1]

Most large departments by this time were operating fire prevention bureaus that inspected public, commercial, and industrial structures on a regular basis. Some departments also operated "arson" bureaus to track down fires of a suspicious nature (not uncommon during the Depression).

The following is an example of the composition of a large city department in the mid-1930s. Michael P. Duffy, Director of Public Safety in Newark, New Jersey, reported:

We have at present 29 engine companies, 12 hook-and-ladder companies, a chemical company, a water-tower company, a fireboat company, and a searchlight company; and the uniformed force consists of 12 chiefs, 90 captains and 600 firemen, totaling 702.

In service are 36 pumping engines, hose cars and boosters, 12 combination chemical and hose cars, 15 aerial hook and ladder trucks, two water towers, one chemical car, one search-light car, one 60-foot steel hull fire-boat, eight chiefs' cars, and 17 other pieces of apparatus, including a wrecker and a fuel and supply car.[2]

Equipment purchases slowed because of the Depression. Unique apparatus purchased by FDNY during this decade were thawing units mounted on 1934 International chassis. The units generated steam that was applied by hose to the frozen hydrants. In 1936 eight more thawing units were added, and these were mounted on GMC chassis. FDNY shops converted two of the 1921 White/Pirsch city service rigs into smoke ejectors. Two Ward La France searchlight trucks were also purchased. Toward the end of the decade, two air compressor trucks were purchased to be used for rescue work. An airport crash rig on a Diamond-T chassis was built for La Guardia Airport, and several old pumpers were outfitted with chemical tanks so they could operate on bridges.

---

[1] *The American City* (February 1932), p. 17.

[2] *The American City* (November 1936), p. 50.

Trucks were now streamlined. Enclosed equipment cabinets became common. In 1938 American-LaFrance delivered a city service ladder truck to Waterloo, Iowa, with the ladders in a completely enclosed compartment that contained all the ladders. The main reason given was that if the ladders got wet in cold weather, they might freeze either to the truck's racks, or ladder sections might freeze together. This was the decade when autos and trucks evolved from box-like shapes into streamlined shapes that were near missile-like. Probably the most attractive motorized fire apparatus of all time was produced and designed during this decade. Especially attractive was the American-LaFrance apparatus of the mid-1930s, and the General of Detroit rigs of the late 1930s. Apparatus mounted on commercial Diamond-T chassis were also very striking in appearance, almost limousine-like.

Electric sirens, usually built by Federal, were used. Rotating or oscillating red warning lights were in widespread use, and they took the place of plain red lens lamps that merely blinked on and off.

Pneumatic tires were now common, as were four-wheel brakes. Some apparatus even used air brakes. Chain drive was gone. Diesel engines were being placed in a few trucks on an almost experimental basis.

The steering wheel was now always on the left. Windshields were provided, even in front of some tiller seats. Doors, semi-enclosed cabs, and fully enclosed cabs were used. High speed accidents proved that it was dangerous for firefighters to be standing on the sides or at the rear of apparatus speeding toward fires. Sedan-type apparatus and sedan-type cabs allowed all firefighters to be seated.

The "quint" came into use during the late 1930s. It combined five functions by carrying a pump, hose, a booster system, ground ladders, and an aerial ladder. The actual market for quints was not large; sometimes they went to small departments that wanted one piece of equipment that "could do everything." San Francisco ran a unique type of equipment known as tank wagons. They carried water and small pumps, and some had high pressure batteries that would have to be supplied water by pumpers. Other San Francisco wagons carried foam generators for use at petroleum fires. San Francisco's tank wagons ran independently of other companies. This would be the last decade that water towers would be built. The hydraulic aerial ladder, with a nozzle at its top, could perform just about the same function. Straight ladder trucks, or city service trucks, also began to receive "lower ratings" from fire insurance companies that evaluated communities' fire departments, which worked to encourage communities to purchase aerial ladders in their place.

Rescue squads began carrying inhalators, which were used for victims of near-drowning and gas inhalation. At the site of fires, they also were used by firefighters who had inhaled too much smoke.

Fire department shops were busy. The Indianapolis shops built a city service truck in 1935 and seven pumps (through 1948). The shop-built pumpers were powered with Hercules engines and had 1937 Diamond-T grilles. The Indianapolis shop also built three tankers and two rescue squads, and rebuilt two Stutz pumpers. They purchased other components from Stutz for use on their builds and rebuilds. Trenton, New Jersey's shops turned out some pumpers during this era. The fire department shops of Beaumont, Texas, built a light truck on a REO commercial chassis, and equipped it with a Westinghouse generator powered by a 29 hp Hercules motor that could generate 14.7 Kilowatts. Some lights were fixed to the truck, but the truck also carried several thousand feet of cable. Shops for the joint department serving Texarkana, Arkansas, and Texarkana, Texas, built a floodlight truck on a GMC chassis. In addition to floodlights, the truck carried one powerful spotlight to penetrate thick smoke.

Toledo studied the feasibility of using its own shops. They noted that:

> Many of the rigs built by [apparatus] manufacturers are assembled from standard parts which can be readily obtained in commercial truck chassis at a lower cost....
>
> The simplest unit to analyze was the ladder truck, which is actually little more that a tool truck with a special body designed to carry the equipment necessary for fire fighting. From an automotive standpoint, almost all the standard truck manufacturers produce chassis which are adequate to meet the requirements. Specifications were drawn to meet those of the manufacturers of fire equipment, and it was found that even with the slight changes which had to be made in commercial chassis, a considerable saving could be effected. In addition, the chassis would be made up of standard motors, axles, clutches, transmissions, etc., any of which could be replaced from local distributors without delay and at low cost.

The first ladder truck was assembled in the shop on a standard commercial chassis by the regular force, without...stopping regular maintenance of equipment in fire houses. [3]

By the end of the decade, Toledo's shops had assembled three city service trucks, one sixty-five-foot aerial ladder, eight 750 gpm pumpers, one service truck, and one rescue squad truck. In addition, they converted tractors on an aerial ladder. They used chassis supplied by Ahrens-Fox, Buffalo, and Schacht.

Some cities, strapped for funds, rebuilt older apparatus since they could afford new equipment. A San Jose department slogan of the era was, "If we can't buy, let's build." San Jose sent its 1914 Gorham-Seagrave pumper to Hall-Scott in Berkeley for a rebuild.

Barton pumps were often used on "build-it-yourself" apparatus and on apparatus built on commercial chassis. Barton pumps were built by the American Steam Pump Company of Battle Creek. At the decade's end, the Auto Body Works of Appleton, Wisconsin (eventually to become Pierce) built its first piece of fire apparatus on a commercial chassis, utilizing a Barton-American pump.

Many cities were strapped for funds and some stations were closed. A study in Boston used to justify station closures compared fire protection costs in that city with other major U.S. cities in 1934. Here are some of the comparisons:[4]

CITY	COST PER			MEN PER		
	sq.mi.	capita	$1000 val	sq.mi.	1000 pop	$ bil.
Boston	$90,600	$5.08	$1.84	37	2.07	918
New York	83,200	3.51	1.17	23	.94	321
San Fran.	80,600	5.27	1.07	28	1.74	682
Buffalo	65,900	4.45	1.84	24	1.56	722
Pittsburgh	49,300	3.72	1.38	16	1.21	688
Milwaukee	47,600	3.30	1.41	19	1.29	690

As Federal public works programs got underway, funds were used to build new municipal buildings, and this included many fire stations. At the decade's end, some cities had two-way radio communication between fire stations, or between departmental headquarters and the chiefs' cars. Telephones became increasingly important as a means of reporting fires. In 1938 San Diego received 138 alarms from its alarm box system, 1,852 by telephone, 206 verbally, and one via sprinkler system activation.[5]

San Francisco used a Public Works Administration grant to add twenty 75,000-gallon cisterns to its emergency water supply system. These subsurface cisterns at various street intersections were kept filled with piped-in water. In case of an earthquake, pumpers would draw water from them. San Francisco also had two salt-water pumping stations that could pump sea water into their fire hydrant system in situations where the municipal water supplies were interrupted.

Ahrens-Fox survived the Depression and also modernized the appearance of its pumpers, still distinctive with the massive globe about their front-mount pump. In 1940 Ahrens-Fox delivered four aerials to FDNY, and these were to be the last aerials the firm built. Big cities buying Ahrens-Fox apparatus during the 1930s included Akron; Boston; Cincinnati; Dayton; Detroit; Hoboken; Kansas City, Missouri; Los Angeles; Louisville; New York

---

[3] *The American City* (June 1941) p. 65.

[4] *The American City* (September 1934), p. 63.

[5] *The American City* (July 1939), p. 77.

City; Newark; Paterson; Pittsburgh; Salt Lake City; San Francisco; Wichita; and Worcester.

In 1931 American-LaFrance introduced its V-12 engine, developing 260 horsepower. The engine was actually two six-cylinder engines with a common crankshaft. FDNY received several orders of American-LaFrance pumpers and Chicago bought six quads. In 1933 American-LaFrance introduced its 300 series and in 1934 and 1935, its 400 series. The 400 "Metropolitan" series looked sleek and powerful because of its long hood containing a V-12 engine. In addition, the pump was mounted in the cowl, making the hood appear even longer. An advantage of the cowl-mounting was that the engine's power could be applied directly to the pump without passing through the truck's transmission. In 1938 Los Angeles created a "super company" system involving the use of manifold wagons. Using American-LaFrance (and other makes) the manifold wagons carried fireboat-size deck turrets and numerous inlets and outlets. Its purpose was to help redistribute water at major fire sites. Manifold wagons ran with American-LaFrance duplex pumpers, which carried two pumps: the cowl mounted pump driven by the truck's engine, and a second pump in the rear, driven by a second engine mounted in the truck's bed. The purpose of the duplex, which could pump three thousand gallons per minute, was to reduce the number of pumpers needed at commercial fires. In the same year, American-LaFrance introduced its series 500, which was as streamlined as most autos of that era. The 500 series provided seats for firefighters and had no running boards. Also at this time, American-LaFrance built its first all-metal hydraulically-lifted aerial ladder. Late in 1938 the firm announced a cab-forward aerial with the engine in front of the axle and a bucket seat on each side of the engine. Over one hundred of these new aerials were sold, with some customers being Atlantic City; Buffalo; Kansas City, Missouri; Lawrence; Ogden; Omaha; Pontiac; San Jose; Stockton; and Union City, New Jersey. Looking backward, it appears that American-LaFrance was leading the industry during the 1930s. Its cab-forward design, which improved the driver's visibility and shortened the necessary wheelbase, was ahead of its time. Eventually the entire industry would follow.

Buffalo apparatus switched from Waukesha to Hercules motors. In the late 1930s, Buffalo began offering an enclosed four-door cab that carried seven firefighters.

Byron-Jackson, a well-known pump builder that supplied many apparatus manufacturers, began building "salvage" pumps that were mounted on four-wheel trailers. They would be parked at the curb after a fire and used to pump water out of the building's basement. The pumps could be pushed for short distances by hand, and were narrow enough to be placed inside structures, often in front of elevator shafts where a suction hose would be dropped into the basement.

W. S. Darley of Chicago, which had originally begun as a catalog firm selling supplies to municipalities, began building some apparatus on commercial chassis, as well as continuing to supply parts for others.

FWD delivered a number of ladder trucks to FDNY, and sold apparatus to many Wisconsin communities.

General of Detroit built some large, very streamlined trucks in the late 1930s and also built on commercial chassis. Several General of Detroit pumpers, built on large Packard commercial (auto) chassis were probably the most elegant-appearing fire engines turned out during this era.

General of St. Louis began building a custom line of apparatus, with their home town of St. Louis apparently being their major customer. The Central Fire Truck Corporation, also of St. Louis, also began building a custom line of rigs.

Kenworth, located in Seattle, made its first delivery of fire apparatus in 1932. The buyer was Sumner, Washington. In the late 1930s, Portland, Oregon, purchased two Kenworth pumpers, a city service truck, and a disaster wagon. In 1940 San Francisco's Fire Department placed a four-wheel drive Hall-Scott powered Kenworth wrecker into service. Also in 1940, a Kenworth quad was delivered to Los Angeles, with a streamlined body built by United Aircraft Company.

The Luverne Automobile Company in Luverne, Minnesota, was outfitting apparatus for smaller communities.

Mack continued to be a major builder of medium and large commercial trucks, and also the builder of reputable fire apparatus. In the mid-1930s Mack delivered a completely enclosed sedan pumper to Charlotte, and in 1938 a batch of Mack sedan pumpers (seating nine firefighters on three seats) were delivered to Chicago. Major U.S. cities bought Mack pumpers and ladder trucks during this era.

Maxim stayed in business, supplying mainly customers in the Northeast. During the 1930s several styling changes were introduced and in 1939 the firm offered a pumper with a four-door sedan-style cab.

The New Stutz firm that H. C. Mecklenburg had founded in 1929 kept busy the entire decade. They built on commercial chassis, and in 1937 New Stutz released a new model pumper, the series A, with a front-end treatment with a wedge looking almost like a high cow-catcher. A "first" for New Stutz was the use of diesel power plant in a pumper. A 175 hp Cummins diesel engine was installed and, in tests, pumped twenty-four hours continuously. Fire chiefs were slow to grasp the diesel's advantages and it took a while for the diesel-powered New Stutz to be sold. It went to Columbus, Indiana, in 1939. As World War II started, the New Stutz plant was converted to the production of aircraft parts, and the firm dropped out of the fire apparatus business.

The Roanoke Welding Company in Roanoke built truck bodies in the 1920s and began outfitting some fire apparatus. In the late 1930s they adopted the name "Oren" for their fire apparatus work which now included both custom apparatus as well as work on commercial chassis.

During the 1930s Pirsch maintained its fine reputation for ladder trucks utilizing aluminum alloy for aerials. Markets for Pirsch were strong in the Midwest and East, and some were sold on the West Coast. Memphis was a very good Pirsch customer.

Seagrave introduced a restyled apparatus in 1935, and in the same year, came out with a V-12 engine and a hydraulically-lifted metal aerial. Interestingly, the engine was nearly identical to the one used in Pierce-Arrow autos, and one-half century later, auto restorers fortunate enough to own a vintage Pierce-Arrow auto can rely on Seagrave for certain engine parts. In the late 1930s, Los Angeles purchased two Seagrave manifold wagons to run with their American-LaFrance Duplex pumpers. In the last half of the decade Seagrave made a number of deliveries of enclosed, sedan-style pumpers.

Walter, a Long Island City firm that still builds all-wheel drive trucks used for snowplows, delivered several tractors to FDNY that were used to pull ladder trucks. Several Walter hose wagons were also supplied.

Ward LaFrance introduced its streamlined models in 1936, featuring a V-grille. Many Ward LaFrance trucks were powered by Waukesha motors and carried Northern or Waterous pumps. FDNY would be Ward LaFrance's best customer. The firm became well known for its airport crash trucks.

Salvage corps cut back their operations because of the Depression. In Baltimore, a 1931 White was purchased, and was the corps' first rig with pneumatic tires. Later in the decade an American-LaFrance was purchased. Boston's corps began using Fords, possibly to save money, although the cabs and rear bodies were now enclosed. In San Francisco, two Internationals were purchased by the salvage corps.

The depression had hit the apparatus builders hard because many communities had to delay their purchases of new equipment. Many manufacturers of truck chassis went out of business during the 1930s. At the end of the 1930s, business and the economy began expanding, in part because of war orders coming from Europe. This would also be the last decade when generous numbers of firefighters were assigned to each station. Pictures of trucks responding to alarms often showed them carrying six to nine firefighters. Insurance underwriters began giving credit for the availability of the "off" platoon, and departments had to make certain that a specified percentage of "off" firefighters would respond within a certain period of time. Additional apparatus had to be provided for the "off" platoons to man; usually this was older apparatus that had been retired from first-line service.[6] A standard mentioned was that "the National Board of Fire Underwriters recommends one pumping engine in reserve for each eight engines in regular service, and one ladder truck in reserve for each five in regular service."[7]

Air raids over London demonstrated how destruction could be dropped from the skies.

> When . . . British Prime Minister Neville Chamberlain returned from his Munich conference with Adolph Hitler, it is said, one of his first moves was to order several thousand trailers, equipped with 100-gpm pumps, and thousands of feet of hose. He had obtained a glimpse of Germany's air power and its ability to distribute incendiary bombs. These bombs weigh only a pound, so that one plane can carry hundreds of them. Such a bomb, dropped at several thousand feet, penetrates a roof and starts an attic fire, one of the most difficult types of fire to extinguish.[8]

By late 1940 both Europe and Asia were engulfed in war. U.S. radio listeners could hear nightly reports of air raids over Europe, and there was great concern that U.S. cities and their fire departments would have difficulty in weathering similar onslaughts.

---

[6] *The American City* (January 1931), p. 77.

[7] *The American City* (May 1936), p. 89.

[8] *The American City* (January 1941), p. 35.

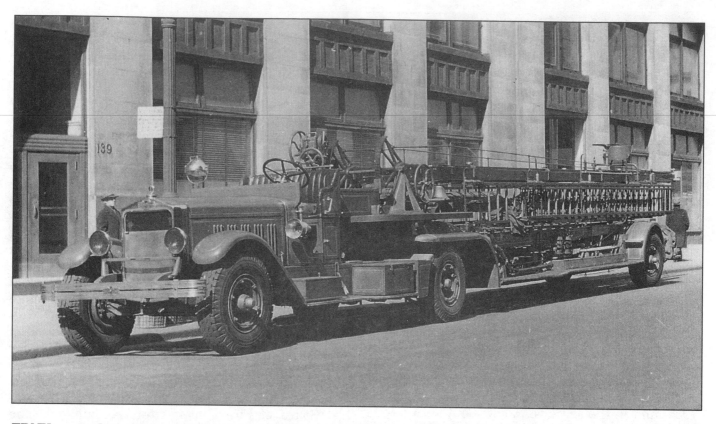

FDNY received ten of these 1931 American-LaFrance Master Series Type 217 seventy-five-foot aerials. Pneumatic tires were added later. (Photo courtesy Jack J. Lerch and Dick Adelman)

In 1931 twenty-one American-LaFrance "Master Series" Type 200, 700 gpm, rotary gear pumpers were delivered to FDNY. Initially they had solid rubber tires, which were later replaced with pneumatic ones. (Photo courtesy Jack J. Lerch and Dick Adelman)

This is FDNY's Engine 91, a 1931 American-LaFrance Type 200, 700 gpm, rotary gear pumper, one of an order of twenty-one. These were the last rotary gear pumpers purchased by FDNY. This one was photographed after a windshield and pneumatic tires were added. (Photo courtesy Frank J. Fenning)

This is Newark, New Jersey's Engine 27, a 1931 American-LaFrance Type 200 Master Series 1000 gpm pumper. Note the wind breaker. Headlights have been replaced with sealed-beam units. (Photo courtesy Dick Adelman)

Princeton, New Jersey, bought this 1931 Buffalo four-tank chemical car for its "Hook & Ladder and Chemical Co. No. 1." Note three hose reels and a large inventory of hand extinguishers. (Photo courtesy Buffalo Fire Appliance Company)

FDNY purchased two 1931 Mack ACs for used as rescue squad trucks. Here is Squad 3 after a roof and pull-down curtains were added in 1940. In front of the spare tire is a foam hopper and generator. (Photo courtesy Jack J. Fenning)

Stroudsburg, Pennsylvania, ran this 1931 Mack aerial truck. Below the ladder bed, cables and turnbuckles are visible, apparently used to keep the body from sagging. Mack aerials during the 1930s had engine-driven ladder hoists rather than devices that relied on springs or hydraulics. The ground ladders rest in a double bank. (Photo courtesy Ernest N. Day)

The Moyamensing Hook and Ladder Company of Chester, Pennsylvania, used this 1931 Mack Type 90 aerial ladder. The truck's 120 hp six-cylinder engine also raised the aerial through use of a power-take-off coupling. (Photo courtesy John J. Robrecht)

Trainer, Pennsylvania, ran this 1931 Mack B Series 500 gpm pumper. Note large hose reel feeding to the rear. Headlights are not original. (Photo courtesy John J. Robrecht)

A 1931 Pirsch with a 600 gpm Hale pump, which ran initially as Engine 2 in Waukesha, Wisconsin, where it was chased by a much younger Don Wood. Wood was thrilled to see it again—fifty years later—at a 1993 Milwaukee Fire Buffs show. (Photo courtesy Don Wood)

This tractor-drawn, eighty-five-foot aerial was built by Seagrave for Cleveland in 1931. The aerial was raised using springs compressed in steel tubes mounted on the turntable, barely visible behind the front seat. (Photo courtesy Seagrave)

This 1931 Pirsch smoke ejector has a very significant history. It was credited by Chicago's Fire Commissioner M. J. Corrigan with saving the lives of sixteen Chicago firemen trapped in a tunnel fire on April 14, 1931. The ejector was used to remove smoke and other fumes. One of the large diameter tubes is visible in the center of the picture. At far right is Peter Pirsch. Ernest N. Day of the New Jersey Fire Equipment Corporation was a one-time Pirsch dealer and recalled that, although the firm was probably best known for developing the metal aerial ladders, Peter Pirsch continued to be interested in the high quality of wood used in ground ladders. The firm purchased the wood in carload lots. Pirsch was stricken and died while inspecting the company's stockpile of ladder lumber. The other picture is from a trade journal with a caption that read: "The new Pirsch smoke ejector saves 16 lives in Chicago." (Photo courtesy Firestone Archives)

In 1931 the Trenton Fire Department shops turned out this 1000 gpm pumper, which ran as Engine 1. Note chain drive, double bumper, and winter windshield. (Photo courtesy John J. Robrecht)

The U.S. Fire Apparatus Company of Wilmington, Delaware, built this 750 gpm pumper for Tallyville, Delaware, in 1931. (Photo courtesy John J. Robrecht)

American-LaFrance delivered six Series 300, 1000 gpm, rotary gear quads to Chicago in 1932. Here we see a heavily-laden Engine 81 carrying 350 feet of ground ladders and a 100-gallon booster tank. (Photo courtesy Stanley Helberg)

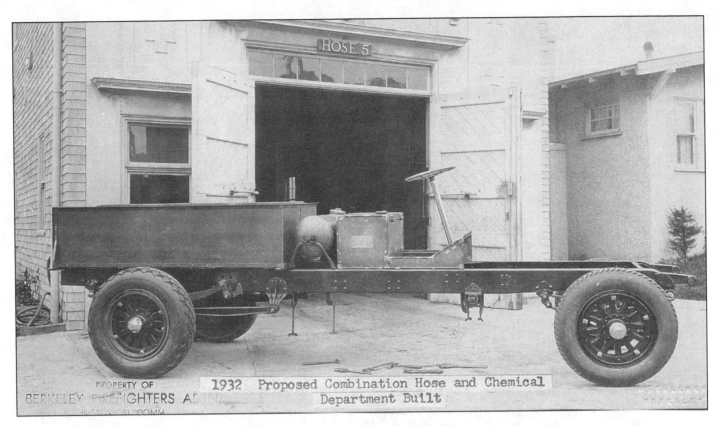

The mechanics of the Berkeley, California, fire department built a combination chemical and hose car in the early 1930s. It is shown here while under construction in 1932, and after completion. The tires, chassis, and Hall-Scott motor were new; all other parts were recycled from older rigs, and at the time of the first photo, total costs were expected to be under $3,000. (Photo courtesy Berkeley Fire Department)

Engine 4 in Fall River, Massachusetts, was this 1932 Maxim 750 gpm triple combination. Note deck gun, chromed hood louvres, and bucket seats. (Photo courtesy Maxim)

Nahant, Massachusetts, operated this circa-1932 Maxim city service truck. Radiator louvre doors were chrome-plated. Note windbreaker. (Photo courtesy Maxim)

Pirsch built this 1932 quad for Fond du Lac, Wisconsin. Note the suction hose on the running board, and the barrel-shaped fuel and water tanks behind the seat. The lengths of ground ladders are stenciled, and one can see lengths of 16, 25, 28, 35, and 50 feet. The unit was powered by a six-cylinder Waukesha engine. (Photo courtesy Pirsch)

An early 1930s Stoughton Community Fire Fighter built in Stoughton, Wisconsin, and sold to Antioch, Illinois. It carried a 500 gpm Northern pump. (Photo courtesy Ed and Ann Bosanko)

This 1932 Seagrave tractor was used to pull a tillered city service trailer, built in the San Francisco Fire Department shops. It ran as Truck 6. (Photo courtesy Paul Darrell)

This 1932 Seagrave water tower was the last water tower that Seagrave produced. It was used by Washington, D.C. Note closely the portrait of George Washington on the truck's hood, in front of a Klaxon-style siren. This model 626 was on a long wheelbase, chain-drive chassis, riding on four solid wheels and solid tires. There is a deck gun toward the rear with four inlets and two outlets. On the running board is an assortment of different style nozzles. The tower was scrapped in 1956. (Photo courtesy Seagrave)

A 1932 Sterling tractor was used in St. Louis, Missouri, to pull Truck 5's eighty-five-foot wooded aerial. (Photo courtesy Paul Paully)

Boston used a 1932 Sterling chassis for Fuel Truck No. 1. It also carried an air compressor. (Photo courtesy Charles E. Beckwith)

This 1933 American-LaFrance 400 Series with a 240 hp V-12 engine was delivered to San Francisco, where the fire department shops added the high pressure and hose body. (Photo courtesy Paul Darrell)

Deal, New Jersey, used a 1933 Diamond-T chassis for its light wagon. Reels hold electric cable. (Photo courtesy Jim Burner)

Wilkes Barre used a 1933 Federal chassis for its floodlight and compressor truck. The floodlights are covered by canvas and there is a turret at the rear. (Photo courtesy John J. Robrecht)

Reading, Pennsylvania's aerial ladder was a 1939 Pirsch 100-foot aluminum alloy with closed lattice design, pulled by an early 1930s Mack B tractor. This truck served the city's Washington Fire Company No. 2. (Photo courtesy John J. Robrecht)

This 1933 photo was taken in Miami in front of the North Miami Avenue Fire Station. The station is a stylish building with bays facing two streets, and a closed door in the center for the chief's buggy. Truck 2 is shown here with seven firemen wearing white shirts and bow ties. This wooden aerial ladder is pulled by an early '30s REO tractor. (Photo courtesy Florida State Archives)

A 1933 Studebaker/Boyer with a 500 gpm front-mount pump used in Masasquan, New Jersey. It also had booster equipment. (Photo courtesy Bill Schwartz)

A circa-1933 Seagrave pumper working at a large fire in New York. (Photo courtesy Charles E. Beckwith)

Here is one of eight 1933 Seagrave 1000 gpm pumpers purchased by FDNY. (Photo courtesy John J. Robrecht)

New York Ladder No. 107 was this 1933 Walter tractor pulling a seventy-five-foot aerial. Note how Walter's engine extends ahead of the front axle, and headlights are cowl-mounted. This truck was delivered with solid tires that were eventually replaced with pneumatic ones. A spare is carried behind the seat. (Photo courtesy Gus Johnson)

Hoboken operated a large fleet of Ahrens-Fox apparatus, including this turret and hose car, which was part of Company 3. It has booster equipment and a mounted turret. (Photo courtesy John J. Robrecht)

One of four 1934 Ahrens-Fox Model N-2 1000 gpm pumpers delivered to FDNY. At this late date, they still had right-hand steering. (Photo courtesy Ahrens-Fox)

A city service truck built by the shops of the Indianapolis Fire Department in 1934-35. It served as Hook & Ladder 5. (Photo courtesy Indianapolis Fire Department)

A 1934 Pirsch tractor was used by Memphis to replace a 1917 American-LaFrance tractor in front of an 1897 Femco water tower. The sixty-foot tower had a long life; in 1956 Pirsch rebuilt it. (Photo courtesy Dick Adelman)

Memphis bought two Pirsch 1000 gpm pumpers in 1934. This one ran with the suction hose preconnected. (Photo courtesy Dick Adelman)

Memphis bought this 1934 Pirsch eighty-five-foot wood aerial. (Photo courtesy Dick Adelman)

A 1934 Studebaker school bus chassis was outfitted by the Port Arthur Ship Building Company in Port Arthur, Ontario, for use as a city service truck in that city's fire department. (Photo courtesy Dan G. Martin)

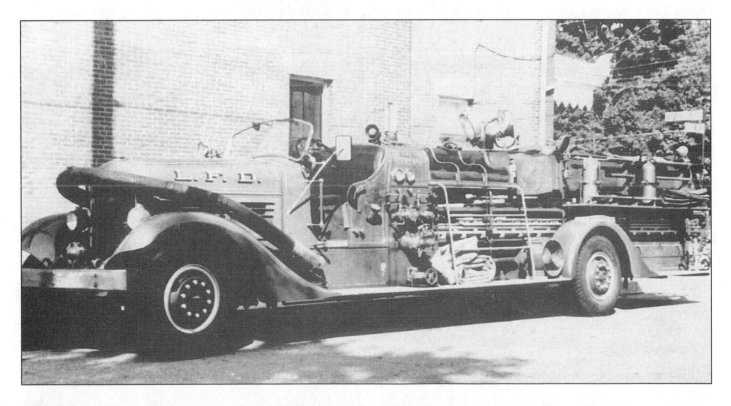

A 1935 Ahrens-Fox quad with a 1000 gpm Hale pump, used in Louisville. Note especially the side-facing seats to the right of the pump. This picture was taken when the truck was close to retirement. It is shown with sealed-beam headlights and "AUX" stenciled above "Quad No. 6." (Photo courtesy Roland Boulet)

Engine 7 in Minneapolis was this 1935 Buffalo with a 1000 gpm Northern pump. (Photo courtesy Walt Schyver)

This 1935 Kenworth city service truck was Spokane's Truck 3. It was built in the department's shops. (Photo courtesy Paccar)

A 1935 GMC tractor in front of an American-LaFrance eighty-five-foot aerial ladder. It ran as Ladder 2 in Jersey City. Note advertising-like sign above windshield saying "Jersey City." This was unusual for fire apparatus. (Photo courtesy Gus Johnson)

Truck 1 in Tacoma was a 1914 Seagrave eighty-five-foot aerial pulled by a 1935 Kenworth tractor that was powered by a Hercules engine. (Photo courtesy Paccar)

Cincinnati's Engine 20 was this 1935 Mack B-Series Type 75 pumper with a 110 hp motor and a 750 gpm pump. (Photo courtesy Mack)

In 1935 Maxim built this 750 gpm centrifugal pumper for Salem, Massachusetts. The mesh box to the right of the pump is a suction hose strainer. The headlights are not original. (Photo courtesy Dan G. Martin)

Charlotte, North Carolina, bought this 1935 Mack "fire sedan," which is believed to be the first enclosed pumper sold in the U.S. This B-Series Mack Type 19 had a 700 gpm pump and could seat ten firefighters. (Photo courtesy Mack)

Sacramento ran this 1935 Seagrave rescue squad. It had numerous equipment compartments. The compartment behind the rear wheel had a reel of electrical wire. Note louvres at two heights. (Photo courtesy Seagrave)

The San Francisco Fire Department shops used a 1935 Seagrave chassis to design and build a high-pressure battery and hose wagon, which ran as Hose Tender 4. (Photo courtesy San Francisco Fire Department)

This impressive rig is a 1936 American-LaFrance V-12 400 city service truck that ran as Ladder 15 in Omaha. Barely visible in the center, behind the fire extinguisher, is a semi-circular wind protector for a standing firefighter. (Photo courtesy Bob Fitz)

This is San Francisco's Tank Wagon 5, a 1936 American-LaFrance 400 Series with a 500 gpm pump and a 350-gallon water tank. It was powered by American-LaFrance's 170 hp V-12 engine. It was the first triple combination in the San Francisco Department. (Photo courtesy Paul Darrell)

Boston's 1936 Ahrens-Fox model BT 1000 gpm pumper. On the back of this factory photo is rubber-stamped:

Ahrens-Fox Fire Engine Co.
New England Sales & Service
15 Mechanic Lane
Taunton, Mass. Tel. 425

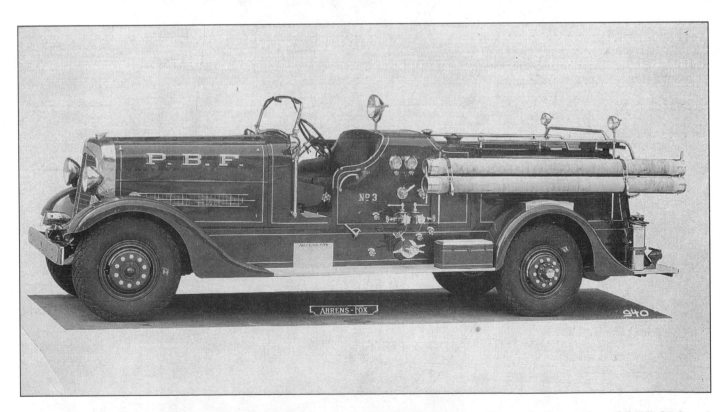

Pittsburgh received the only 1250 gpm rotary gear pump built by Ahrens-Fox. It was designated model BR-SPC and was delivered in 1936. (Photo courtesy Ahrens-Fox)

Danvers, Massachusetts, used this 1936 Chevrolet that had a 500 gpm front-mount pump and fixed turret. Above the windshield a sign proclaims: "FIRE." (Photo courtesy Charles E. Beckwith)

Muskegan Heights, Michigan, used a 1936 Chevrolet to build a turret wagon. Handwheels are used to aim the turret, and three inlets are visible above the hose box. (Photo courtesy Dan G. Martin)

Gerstenslager Corporation of Wooster, Ohio, built a rescue squad body for Omaha using a 1936 Diamond-T chassis. (Photo courtesy Omaha Fire Department)

The Chrysler and DeSoto "Airflow" cars were ahead of their time and did not sell well. Chrysler also introduced Dodge Airflow trucks, which were used mainly to carry streamlined petroleum tank bodies. Here are two views of a 1936 Dodge Airflow used by a rescue squad in Teaneck, New Jersey. Considerable equipment was carried. (Photos courtesy Dick Adelman)

One of twelve 1936 FWD ladder trucks delivered to FDNY. The wooden aerial was eighty-five feet long. (Photo courtesy John J. Robretch)

The correctional facility in Elmira, New York, used a 1936 International C Series to build a small tanker with a mounted turret. The sign on the rear says that the rig had been reconditioned by the institution's auto body class. (Photo courtesy Dick Adelman)

This unique rig was designed and built in the Indianapolis Fire Department shops in 1936. It ran as Engine 7 and carried a 1000 gpm pump. (Photo courtesy Indianapolis Fire Department)

Baltimore's Hook and Ladder 26 was this 1936 BQ Mack 750 gpm quad. (Photo courtesy Wayne Sorensen)

One of twenty 1936 Mack Type 21, 1000 gpm pumpers delivered to FDNY. The deck monitors were controlled by hand cranks. (Photo courtesy Dick Adelman)

A 1936 New Stutz on a commercial chassis delivered to Altoona, Pennsylvania. (Photo courtesy Lynn Sams Collection)

A 1936 Pirsch converted from a pumper to a foam wagon. It carries foam in the hose bed, and in the front and back of the rear wheel we see hopper funnels (upside down) used to feed foam powder into hose line. Headlights and grille are not original. Note the two handwheel-controlled mounted monitors. (Photo courtesy Walt Scheyver)

Harrisburg, Pennsylvania, operated this 1936 REO combination hose and chemical car. It had two chemical tanks. (Photo courtesy John J. Robrecht)

Seagrave referred to this as a "limousine" pumper, and delivered four of them in 1936 to Detroit, where they were nicknamed "pie wagons" because they looked like the enclosed trucks used by bakeries. They had V-12 motors and 700 gpm pumps, and were designated as Models JW-440T. (Photo courtesy Seagrave)

This is an early military airfield crash truck built by the Army Quartermaster Corps at Fort Holabird, Maryland, in the mid-1930s. Both rear axles are powered on this Type Q unit. The unit carried foam, a 500 gpm pump, and booster equipment. A foam hopper is visible on the running board. (Photo courtesy George C. Marshall Foundation)

In 1937, Memphis upgraded its water tower, which consisted of a 1018 American-LaFrance Type 31 two-wheel tractor placed in front of a fifty-five-foot water tower built by Hale in 1897. The tower could deliver 7000 gpm. Modifications in 1937 included the addition of a "crow's nest," pneumatic rear wheels, and a windshield. (In 1956 a four-wheel 1934 Pirsch tractor would replace the American-LaFrance.) The tower was retired after seventy-five years of service, and was the last of 115 water towers in fire service in the U.S. (Photo courtesy Dick Adelman)

Salt Lake City's Engine 2 was this 1937 Ahrens-Fox HC 1000 gpm pumper. Note streamlined, enclosed cab, and pump controls. (Photo courtesy Ahrens-Fox)

This is one of five 1937 American-LaFrance Series 400, 1500 gpm pumpers that Los Angeles purchased. Pump is in cowl. Note four door crew cab. These engines were affectionately referred to as "Lulabelle" by the firefighters. (Photo courtesy American-LaFrance)

This 1937 custom Buffalo 750 gpm pumper with an enclosed sedan body was used in Winona, Minnesota. Enclosed-cab apparatus was especially popular in cold climates. Note bell tower. (Photo courtesy John Gambs)

This is San Francisco's Tank Wagon 7, a 1937 Fageol that was quartered with Truck 11. This wagon carried 450 gallons of water and had a 90 gpm pump, plus a foam generator and hopper. (Photo courtesy John Graham)

General of St. Louis shifted its operations to Detroit. It came out with an attractive line of custom apparatus marketed under the name "General Monarch." The firm's custom units were mounted on chassis built by Available Truck of Chicago. Here is Paducah's 750 gpm triple combination pumper, which ran as Engine 5. (Photo courtesy General of St. Louis)

The fire department shops in San Antonio took this 1937 Hug Model 23 AS chassis and installed a pump and body. (Photo courtesy Chuck Rhodes, who is now restoring this truck)

This 1937 Hahn has a low appearance and almost looks overloaded. It ran in Bath, Pennsylvania. An overhead ladder rack was uncommon. (Photo courtesy Dick Adelman)

New York City's first enclosed cab pumpers were these 1937 Macks. The door is cut to fit around the pump. At the rear is a second windshield and subway-type straps for the crew. To the rear of the single rear wheel is a spare tire. Barely visible above the cab roof is a deck gun. (Photo courtesy Mack)

This 1937 Pirsch 100-foot aerial ladder served Memphis. The aluminum ladder had three sections. It carried a small generator and flood lights. It is pictured in reserve status and has a shop-added cab roof. (Photo courtesy Dick Adelman)

A 1937 Pirsch 1250 gpm triple combination pumper used in Memphis. This engine had a suction hose that was preconnected and carried in squirrel-tail fashion. In front note the rack carrying the bell, with a Mars light on top and siren below, common to Pirsch apparatus. The cab top is shop-built. (Photo courtesy Dick Adelman)

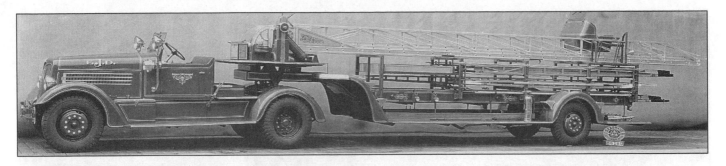

Johnstown, Pennsylvania, operated this 1937 Seagrave aerial. The tiller seat (basket) came with a windshield and windshield wiper, and would swing to the side before the ladder was raised. (Photo courtesy Seagrave)

Ladder 1 in Pocatello was this 1937 Seagrave with a sixty-five-foot aerial. The grille style was nicknamed "sweetheart." (Photo courtesy Wayne Sorensen)

The Aetna Hook and Ladder Company of Newark, Delaware, had its 1921 Stutz 750 gpm pumper rebuilt by New Stutz in about 1937. Part of the rebuild included new front sheet metal. (Photo courtesy New Stutz)

A circa-1937 New Stutz. Note the newly designed front end, especially the lattice-type bumper. (Photo courtesy American Automobile Manufacturers Association)

Fageol and Kenworth pumpers being tested in Portland, Oregon, in 1938. (Photo courtesy Wayne Sorensen Collection)

In 1938, Los Angeles bought this American-LaFrance Series 400 city service truck, which also carried a sixty-five-foot water tower. It has a four-door cab. This was the last water tower built. In the late 1940s, the trailer was converted to carry a water tower only. (Photo courtesy American-LaFrance)

A 1938 American-LaFrance Series 400 manifold wagon built for Los Angeles. The manifold wagon ran with Duplex pumpers, which supplied the wagon with water. The wagon would be positioned at the fire site. The wagon's rear hose bed carried 3-1/2-inch hose, used to feed inlets at the rear. The transverse hose racks carried 2-1/2-inch hose to be connected to the sixteen outlets, eight of which are visible on this side. The unit also carried a small booster tank and small pump. A large deck turret was installed after the unit was delivered. (Photo courtesy American-LaFrance)

In June 1938 American-LaFrance introduced its 500 Series. As part of its streamlined design, the suction hose was placed inside the body, and ladders were carried in an overhead rack. The pump is mounted in the cowl. Reno used this 1250 gpm pumper as Engine 3. During its life it was badly damaged by a bomb and then restored. (Photo courtesy American-LaFrance)

Los Angeles used this 1938 American-LaFrance Type 400 TB city service truck/tractor as Truck 22. The tillered trailer carried a double bank of ladders. Power came from a V-12, 240 hp engine. (Photo courtesy American-LaFrance)

The co-authors of this book spent endless hours sifting through stacks of pictures attempting to select those that were both of high quality and representative of the wide range of apparatus built. During one such meeting, one of the co-authors saw this picture and exclaimed: "This is what a fire engine should look like!" Shown is Brigham City, Utah's 1938 American-LaFrance with a 500 gpm pump and overhead ladder racks. (Photo courtesy John F. Sytsma)

This is one of FDNY's twenty Ahrens-Fox pumpers delivered in 1938. They had single rear wheels and carried a spare tire. Note enclosed cab, deck gun, deck gun inlets, and windshield at rear in front of the rack of subway straps. (Photo courtesy Ahrens-Fox)

FDNY ordered twenty Ahrens-Fox Model HT, 1000 gpm piston pumpers, which were delivered in 1938. This was the largest single order Ahrens-Fox ever received. Here we see Engine 270 pumping at a fire. (Photo courtesy Dick Adelman)

In 1938 the Indianapolis Fire Department shops used Diamond-T chassis to build two rescue squads. Part of their equipment included booster tanks and PTO-powered Boyer booster pumps. When this photo was taken, the rig was in reserve status. (Photo courtesy Dan Martin)

Los Angeles used this 1938 American-LaFrance 400 Series manifold wagon, which ran with a Duplex pumper. It carried a fireboat-size monitor that was fed directly through the manifold. Note intake fittings. The manifold wagon received water from a Duplex pumper and distributed the water to where it was needed at the fire site. It also carried a small booster pump and tank. This unit retired in 1964. (Photo courtesy Dale Magee)

Los Angeles used several impressive 1938 American-LaFrance Series 400 Duplex pumpers. The pump in the cowl was rated at 1500 gpm and was powered by the truck's engine. The rear pump had similar capacity and was powered by a second engine mounted in the rear of the truck. In the picture of the pumper at work, note all the hood doors open for cooling. (Photos courtesy Dale Magee)

A Thornton axle conversion kit was used to give this 1938 Ford two powered rear axles, and American-LaFrance fire fighting equipment was added to make it a combination pumper/crash wagon for use at airports.

In 1938 Savage & Company of Portland, Oregon, built for Portland five 1000 gpm pumpers using Fageol chassis. At the front of the hose bed is a monitor. The rigs were powered by Hall-Scott 175 hp engines. This is Engine 2. (Photo courtesy Jim T. Boyd)

This 1938 Fagcol saw service as San Francisco's Tank Wagon 13. It was built in the department's shops and equipment included a 400-gallon tank, a 90 gpm Viking pump, and a Gorter High Pressure battery. Power came from a Hall-Scott, six-cylinder, 175 hp engine. (Photo courtesy San Francisco Fire Department)

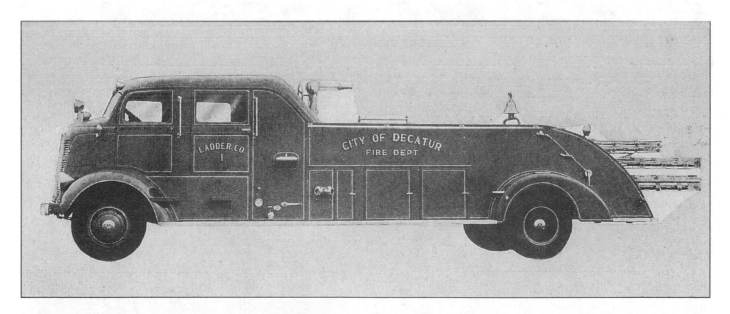

A 1938 GMC COE chassis used by General of Detroit to build a city service truck for Decatur, Illinois. Note the four-door enclosed cab and the turret. (Photo courtesy General of Detroit)

In 1938 Hall-Scott in Berkeley rebuilt San Jose's 1914 Gorham-Seagrave pumper. Within the ranks of the department, the rebuilt rig was known as "white elephant," and it was kept hidden away until its retirement in 1947. (Photo courtesy San Jose Fire Department)

Sound Beach, Connecticut, used a 1938 GMC chassis for its emergency truck.

This is one of two Kenworth all-wheel drive units — powered by Hall-Scott model 177, six-cylinder, 220 hp engines — purchased in 1938 for use in Portland, Oregon. The 1000 gpm pump has already been installed on this one and it is waiting for the body to be added by Wentworth and Irwin of Portland. (Photo courtesy Paccar)

A 1938 Mack 750 gpm quad shown in second-line status in Baltimore. The hood and the bottom were painted red; the remainder of the truck was painted white. (Photo courtesy Wayne Sorensen)

A 1938 Maxim city service truck with a single bank of ladders used in Falmouth, Massachusetts. It has booster equipment and a turret pipe. (Photo courtesy Wayne Sorensen)

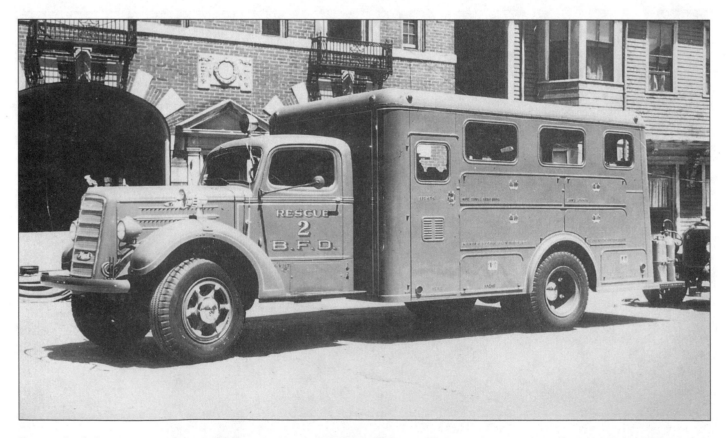

Boston had this rescue body mounted on a circa-1938 Mack E Series chassis. Compartments along the side held portable lighting units and radio equipment. (Photo courtesy Charles E. Beckwith)

Chicago's Engine 22 was this 1938 Mack Type 21, with a Hale 1000 gpm pump and a nine-man cab. It was powered by a Hercules engine. (Photo courtesy Wayne Sorensen)

The airport at Kansas City, Missouri, used this circa-1938 Mack as a crash truck. Compartments held a foam generator (powered by a separate gasoline engine), CO_2 tanks, breathing masks, first aid supplies, and clean-up materials. The chassis was a Mack "E" and was powered by a Mack Thermodyne engine. (Photo courtesy Dick Adelman)

This is Baltimore's 1938 Mack Type 21, 750 gpm triple combination pumper. It was painted red and white, and ran as Engine 53. (Photo courtesy John J. Robrecht and Dick Adelman)

A 1938 New Stutz Model A 500 gpm pumper built for Geneva, Pennsylvania.

A rear view of one of two 1938 Seagrave manifolds purchased by Los Angeles. We see hose compartments, inlets and outlets, and a deluge gun. At large working fires, these units would be strategically located and would take the place of several conventional engine companies. This unit was intended to be supplied by an accompanying American-LaFrance Duplex pumper. (Photo courtesy George "Smoky" Bass)

Trenton's Truck 1 was this 1938 Pirsch Model 16 100-foot, three-section mechanical ladder, sometimes known as the Pirsch "senior" tractor-drawn aerial. (Photo courtesy John J. Robrecht and Dick Adelman)

A 1938 Seagrave manifold wagon in service as Engine 3 in Los Angeles. It carried a large monitor as well as a small booster tank and booster line. This one was assigned to Engine 17. (Photo courtesy Paul Darrell Collection)

A 1938 White chassis carrying a light unit, operated in Charlotte, North Carolina. (Photo courtesy John J. Robrecht)

A collection of apparatus and streams of water at a church fire in New York City, 1939. In front center is a water tower. (Photo courtesy Gus Johnson)

Circa-1939 American-LaFrance Series 500 used by Denver as Engine 12. The pump is mounted in the cowl, with an advantage being a direct connection to the engine without slippage through a transmission. The three small lights above the cab rotate. This device is called a Buckeye Roto Rays. (Photo courtesy American-LaFrance)

In 1939 American-LaFrance introduced its cab-forward design, which would eventually be adopted by all apparatus builders. This model JO/JOX had a seventy-five-foot aerial ladder and went to Union City, New Jersey. A V-12, 190 hp engine powered the unit. A stabilizer jack is concealed midship, and a running board and handle grip extend the length of the rear. (Photo courtesy American-LaFrance)

This 1939 Ahrens-Fox Model H-85 was built for San Francisco. The tractor was powered by a six-cylinder Hercules 225 hp motor. The eighty-five-foot Basque aerial ladder was lifted electronically, relying on banks of batteries to activate and power a hydraulic system. The truck first saw service in 1939 in San Francisco at the 1939-1940 Golden Gate International Exposition, a world's fair that attracted ten million visitors. The truck then became San Francisco's Truck 13. (Photo courtesy Paul Darrell)

The Underwriters' Fire Patrol in Kansas City, Missouri, used this 1939 Chevrolet panel truck. Behind the ladder on top of the truck, note the clean, folded tarpaulins in the rack on the wall. (Photo courtesy Dick Adelman and Murray Young)

A 1939 GMC/Pirsch hose wagon used in Richmond, Virginia, where it ran as part of Engine 8. Roto Rays lights are mounted high behind the cab and in front of the turret. (Photo courtesy Pirsch)

Milwaukee's Heil Co., which built many streamlined gasoline tank trucks during the 1930s, outfitted this airport crash body for Newark, New Jersey, on a 1939 GMC chassis. Rear view shows a collection of CO_2 chemical containers, two reels of different hose, conventional hose racks above the wheels, and two tanks. The unit could deliver streams of water or of chemicals. This was assigned to Engine 35, and was one of the early airport crash trucks. (Photos courtesy The Heil Co.)

GENERAL *Custom Built*

This sleek custom four-door cab, 750 gpm pumper was built in 1939 by General of Detroit for Madison, Wisconsin, where it served as Engine 4. (Photo courtesy General of Detroit)

Mankato, Minnesota, had its fire department shops build this deluge-hose wagon No. 3 using a 1939 International Series D chassis. The truck also carried considerable lighting equipment. (Photo courtesy Walt Schryver)

The United Fire Engine Company built this 500 gpm quad for Los Angeles using a 1939 Kenworth COE chassis powered by a six-cylinder Hall-Scott engine. It was assigned to Truck 39. (Photo courtesy Paccar)

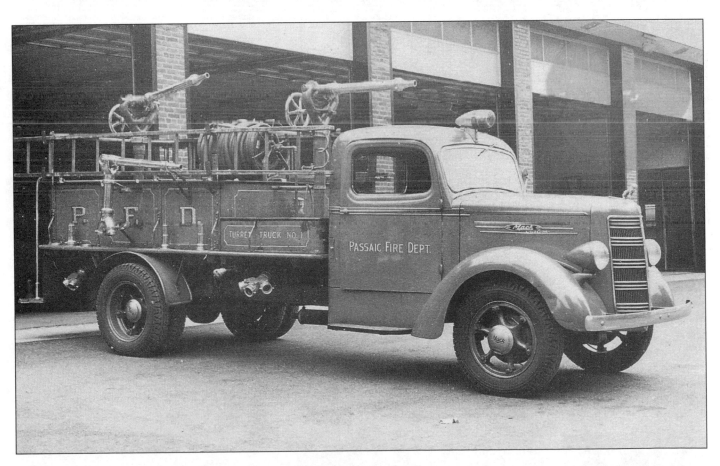

Passaic, New Jersey, used a circa-1939 Mack chassis to built Turret Truck No. 1, which carries two large monitors. Inlets are below the truck bed. (Photo courtesy Dick Adelman)

Joplin, Missouri's Engine 3 was this 1939 Mack E Series, 750 gpm triple combination. It has an enclosed, extended coupe cab. The suction hose is carried in squirrel-tail style. (Photo courtesy Dick Adelman)

This 1939 Maxim with a streamlined canopy cab ran as Milton, Pennsylvania's Engine 4. The pump was rated at 750 gpm. (Photo courtesy Charles E. Beckwith)

In an effort to save money, this 1939 1000 gpm pumper was built in FDNY shops. It had an American-LaFrance pump, a Hercules engine, and Ward LaFrance body work. Note futuristic design. This unit ran as Engine 324. The experiment proved to be costly, and the rig cost more than a comparable unit supplied by existing builders. (Photo courtesy R. Hardy)

Today, most fire apparatus is diesel-powered. Diesel engines are more durable, have fewer moving parts, and are cheaper to operate. The first diesel fire engine in the U.S. was this 1939 New Stutz, which was outfitted with a 175 hp Cummins Diesel Engine. It was used in Columbus, Indiana, and the department there was reluctant to accept it despite the fact that it had passed rigorous tests. The pumper was later rebuilt by Boyer Fire Apparatus in Logansport, Indiana. (Photo courtesy Wayne Sorensen Collection)

Often called the "first Peterbilt," this truck is a 1939 Challenger 500 gpm pumper on a chassis assembled by Peterbilt. The front-end sheet metal and cowl were supplied by Diamond-T. Power came from a Hall-Scott model CH5 motor. It ran in Fremont, California. (Photo courtesy Wayne Sorensen)

A 1939 or 1940 Seagrave. At top are Buckeye Roto Rays red warning lights. The three lights rotate, and at night they look like a glowing red donut. The grille style was nicknamed "waterfall." (Photo courtesy Seagrave)

This Pirsch Model 16, 100-foot aluminum alloy aerial went to Joplin, Missouri, in 1939. A life net is carried below the aerial ladder. Note controls for the ladder's hydro-mechanical hoist. (Photo courtesy Dick Adelman)

This is a 1939 Stewart/Buffalo "Metropolitan" used in Washington, D.C. This 750 gpm pumper was one of twelve ordered. It ran as Engine 26. (Photo courtesy Buffalo Fire Appliance Co.)

Ward LaFrance delivered twenty 1000 gpm pumpers to FDNY during 1939. This one was Engine 30. Note deck gun. Behind it we see a Mack hose wagon. (Photo courtesy Dick Adelman)

Parked here is a 1940 Autocar/U.S. Fire Apparatus open seat pipe line No.4 in service in Philadelphia. The unit carries two large mounted turrets. Notice the short windshield and Roto Rays warning lights. (Photo courtesy John J. Robrecht)

This circa-1940 American-LaFrance four-section, 100-foot aerial went to Cleveland, Ohio. The 500 Series crew cab resulted in a very long rig. Because the ladder had four sections, it was sufficiently short to allow the tiller seat to be fixed. (Photo courtesy American-LaFrance)

This is a 1940 Autocar/U.S. Fire Apparatus pipe line unit was converted to a special deluge unit in the 1950s. The unit carries a large hydraulically-operated Stang Giant turret gun and two portable Eastman-type monitors. (Photo courtesy John J. Robrecht)

This is Turret Wagon 12 operating in St. Louis. It is built on a circa-1940 Central Fire Truck, originally built in that same city. Turret nozzle is the size used on fireboats. (Photo courtesy Robert Pauly)

Some of the biggest fire apparatus in terms of weight were tank trucks used to carry water. Newfane, New York, ran a homebuilt tanker on a 1940 Ford chassis with two rear axles. From what we can see, the truck carried only water, and no other fire fighting gear.

FABCO of Emeryville, California, built the chassis for this 1940 Tank Wagon used as San Francisco's Tank 9. Tank wagons responded as called, and this one carried a 400-gallon water tank, a small pump, and a Gorter high-pressure battery. (Photo courtesy San Francisco Fire Department)

This 1940 FABCO served in San Francisco as a tank wagon. It carried 415 gallons of water and had a 90 gpm Viking pump. (Photo courtesy Paul Darrell)

The San Francisco Bureau of Equipment ran this 1940 Kenworth wrecker, which had a fifteen-ton capacity. The wrecker was powered by a six-cylinder Hall-Scott 175 hp engine. (Photo courtesy Wayne Sorensen)

Lindenhurst, New York, ran this rescue unit with closed equipment compartments built on a 1940 Mack E Series chassis with a Type 45 body. (Photo courtesy Dick Adelman)

A partially-finished Seagrave aerial ladder truck, circa 1940. This was a forerunner of today's much more sophisticated aerial equipment. (Photo courtesy Seagrave)

This 1940 Seagrave 1000 gpm pumper retained the styling that had been adopted in 1935. Abilene, Texas, bought this rig. The hood scroll says "1940." The near headlight has a red lens. The grille style was called "sweetheart." (Photo courtesy Seagrave)

San Jose's 1922 Stutz was rebuilt by Hall-Scott in 1940. A Peterbilt front end was used in the rebuild effort. It has a 750 gpm pump and a 400 gallon round water tank. (Photo courtesy Chris Cavette Collection)

The Army Quartermaster Corps at Fort Holabird, Maryland, built this U.S.A. Type 50 combination 750 gpm pumper for use at army bases. At the war's end it was sold as surplus to Woodlawn, Maryland. (Photo courtesy Dick Adelman)

Philadelphia operated this 1940 Ward LaFrance 1000 gpm triple combination. There is a low windshield and the booster hose is carried in a basket. (Photo courtesy John J. Robrecht)

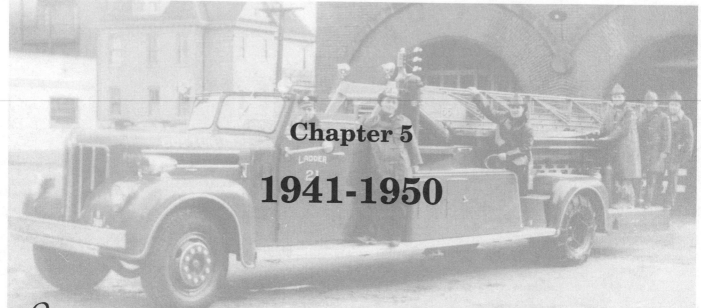

Chapter 5
1941-1950

Once the United States entered the war in late 1941, civilian distribution of trucks ceased and it became very difficult for municipal fire departments to obtain new apparatus. The War Production Board gave top priority to military needs, and then the needs of communities with vital defense industries. Any new apparatus built had no chrome. Brass and bronze, also important to fire departments, were in short supply. In 1943, Philadelphia reported that "six more rescue squads have been organized and, because new trucks are unobtainable, equipped with second-hand trucks we have purchased."[1] As another example of the composition of a large city department, the following is a roster of Philadelphia's other equipment in 1943: one chief engineer's car, sixteen other cars for officers, seventy engines, twenty-eight 85-foot aerial ladder trucks, five pipe-line units equipped with 3-1/2-inch hose for use in high-value districts, eight emergency crew trucks, three water towers, and three fireboats. The engine companies carried 118,000 feet of 2-1/2-inch hose; 14,000 feet of 1-1/2-inch hose; and 24,500 feet of smaller hose. The pipeline companies carried 6,000 feet of 3-1/2-inch hose and the fireboats carried 1,000 feet of 3-1/2-inch hose, plus 1,200 feet of smaller hose. Actual holdings of hose were nearly twice these totals since half of a company's hose would be hanging in hose towers.[2]

Auxiliary Civil Defense fire fighting groups were formed to assist regular fire departments. They trained on a weekly basis, but for the most part, were expected to use the municipality's existing apparatus. Individuals were supplied with helmets, armbands, and overalls. Industrial plants also beefed up their own fire fighting capabilities. A concern of theirs was fires set by saboteurs. Many of the civil defense fire fighting auxiliaries were organized at manufacturing plants, and received special training for handling fires in whatever types of materials were present. Industrial fire brigades played an important role in the nation's defense effort, mainly because they were already on the scene of routine fires at their plants.

One type of equipment that was built for Civil Defense work was trailer-mounted pumpers, consisting of a small pump, suction and discharge hose, fire extinguishers, shovels, and a few other fire fighting tools. Shovels were important because the only way to extinguish an ignited incendiary bomb was to shovel dirt on top of it. Stockpiles of sand were made available and homeowners were advised to keep several buckets of sand and a shovel in their attics so that they could fight incendiary bombs.

Rochester, New York, modified nine of its 2,500 gallon street flushers so that they could also function as emergency pumpers.[3] Cities also negotiated mutual aid pacts with surrounding communities. This included acquisition of adapters to provide universal hose and hydrant couplings. Rochester also provided additional

---

[1] *The American City* (April 1943), p. 60.

[2] Ibid.

[3] *The American City* (September 1943), p. 91

training to the members of the volunteer departments.

Most of the fire fighting trailers and some of the auxiliary apparatus mounted on commercial chassis were paid for by the Federal Office of Civil Defense, and were referred to as OCD equipment. Useful as it was, it was not considered as "first rate" by big city chiefs, and at the war's end they said it should be shipped out of the country or to small places and rural regions for new fire squads where organized fire protection did not formerly exist.

The principal concern was that a bombing attack would result in tens or hundreds of simultaneous fires at different sites. Municipal departments were neither equipped nor manned to be able to cover a large number of small fires. Hence, trailer-mounted pumps provided more equipment, and volunteers and auxiliaries provided manpower (and womanpower). Another concern was establishing alternate, or "back-up" communications systems. There was fear that a single bomb might knock out a department's alarm and communications center. Municipal water mains were also vulnerable to bombing attacks.

Additional heavy rescue equipment was added to many engines and trucks. It was feared that, after a bomb attack, there would be a major need to rescue persons from the rubble. During the 1940s, Chicago operated ten rescue squads, using enclosed Mack trucks.

> The squad units carry a crew of seven men who ride comfortably in the large cab, which is equipped with lockers holding all varieties of life saving apparatus. In addition to the first aid and entry equipment, the trucks are equipped with turret nozzles capable of shooting 1,000 gallons of water a minute, so that each truck can be used directly against the fire while its crew is performing rescue work.[4]

In 1944 the ten squads made a total of 17,237 runs.

San Jose's experiences during World War II provide an example of the war effort. A total of 776 auxiliary firemen were recruited and trained, and they came from thirty-eight industrial plants in the San Jose area. They were trained to control industrial fires before the municipal department arrived. During World War II these San Jose auxiliaries handled a total of 239 fires, and in ninety-five percent of the these they managed to have the fire extinguished before the municipal fire department arrived. During the war, San Jose managed to obtain three pieces of new apparatus: a 1942 Seagrave aerial and two experimental John Bean fog units. An American-LaFrance pumper ordered just before the War was delivered in 1946.

In New York, as part of the civil defense effort, a number of skid-mounted pumps were purchased. In addition, five old aerials were converted to hose carriers carrying 3,000 feet of 3-1/2-inch hose to be used in situations where bombs might destroy water mains. "To make these apparatus less of a target for enemy air attack, they were painted a dull gray and their headlights were blacked out."[5] A traveling laboratory was placed in a standup delivery van for use in analyzing gases and fumes, possibly resulting from an enemy attack. After the war, large orders were placed for new apparatus. In 1947 an old rig was converted to a foam truck, and in 1948 a truck was equipped to carry oxygen tanks. In 1949 a Flxible bus was equipped to serve as a small, mobile hospital.

During the war, new apparatus had been built for and delivered to military installations. As these installations closed down, this apparatus was declared surplus, and many pieces of it were sold to nearby communities. One new type of apparatus was the airport crash truck. Many were bought by the military for use at training fields. They carried foam, fog, or Cardox (pressurized CO_2) equipment, plus some rescue equipment, and asbestos-lined suits for use in rescues. At the war's end, these rigs were turned over to civilian departments.

During this period, Ahrens-Fox ceased its production of fire apparatus. Instead, its plant was used by its parent company, Le Blond, to produce heavy machine tools needed for the war effort. After the war, the company returned to the fire apparatus market in a slow manner, delivering only three pumpers in 1946. A new series was designed and introduced, which had a more conventional truck appearance, including boxed front fenders. Credit for the design goes to Curt Nepper, the chief engineer for Ahrens-Fox. Limited production also continued on the more tradi-

---

[4] *The American City* (August 1945), p. 15.

[5] John A. Calderone and Jack Lerch. *Wheels of the Bravest, a History of FDNY Fire Apparatus, 1865-1982* (Howard Beach, NY: 1984), p. 112.

tional H-T piston pumper, with four going to New Orleans in 1948. Ahrens-Fox had a good year in 1949 when it delivered twenty-six pieces of apparatus.

American-LaFrance supplied numerous 500 series pumpers to the army and the navy. They also made some military deliveries of aerial ladder trucks and of airport crash trucks built on commercial chassis. Some of these crash trucks were truck tractor-tank trailer foam units with remotely controlled foam nozzles, one in front and one on top. (In 1950 American-LaFrance received what would turn into an order for 1,100 Air Force crash trucks.) In common with many manufacturers during the war, American-LaFrance also had defense contracts for building non-related items. In American-LaFrance's case the unrelated items were tail gun mounts used in Army Air Corps bombers. At the war's end, American-LaFrance was ahead of most of its competitors. In terms of design, its cab-forward 700 series, introduced in 1947, would eventually be copied by the entire industry. The 700 series was designed by John Grybos and its cab had room for three firemen in the front seat, and two rearward-facing seats, one on each side of the engine. Orders for its cab-forward pumpers and aerials came in from most large cities such as Boston, Cleveland, New York, and San Francisco.

During this decade, many Autocar truck chassis, built in Ardmore, Pennsylvania, were outfitted as pumpers. Much of the work was done by the U.S. Fire Apparatus Company of Wilmington, Delaware. Philadelphia placed a large order. At the decade's end, Chicago bought eight Autocar cabovers that had four-door cabs and a catwalk to the rear.

FABCO, an Emeryville, California, firm that had built a handful of custom apparatus before the war, received several huge orders for outfitting fire apparatus for military use on Dodge commercial chassis.

FMC's John Bean high pressure fog units were sold as airport crash trucks. Most John Bean units were PTO-powered and utilized a large belt attached to the pump pulley. This gave them the nickname "rubber-band" pumper. Many of the pumper trucks that FMC outfitted had both high pressure fog and regular pumping capabilities.

Buffalo turned out apparatus for the military, but shut down its apparatus line in 1948, deciding to concentrate instead on the production of fire extinguishers. The Young Fire Equipment Corporation of Buffalo, another fire apparatus builder, took over the servicing arrangements for existing Buffalo rigs.

The Central Truck Company of St. Louis delivered eight pumpers to St. Louis in the 1940s, built on GMC chassis. The firm also built some apparatus on Available chassis (which were made in Chicago).

In Los Angeles, Crown Coach Corporation, a truck and bus body builder since 1904, entered into the custom apparatus market in 1949 with its Firecoach, delivered to Covina, a Los Angeles suburb. At this time, Crown was best known for its school buses, and the cab-forward Firecoach had some similarities to their bus design. Crown apparatus were bolted, rather than welded, which made replacement of parts and panels much easier. Crown would develop the reputation as quality, high price apparatus, and the Los Angeles city and Los Angeles county fire department would eventually buy over 270 Crowns. Many movies and TV shows filmed in the Los Angeles area will show Crowns if they have any fire fighting scenes.

FWD in Clintonville was busy turning out heavy-duty all-wheel-drive trucks for military use. At the war's end they filled orders for several northern cities such as Chicago, Newark, and Boston. FWD chassis were also used by other outfitters, such as Darley, because of their rugged off-road capability.

During the war, Howe delivered just under one thousand pumpers to the military to be used for base protection. They also built two thousand trailers with pumps for use by the Office of Civil Defense, and for shipment to England. After the war, Howe built three hundred pieces of fire fighting apparatus based on "Jeeps."

Kenworth made a number of apparatus deliveries in Southern California during the 1940s, working through its dealer, the United Fire Engine Company of Los Angeles, which also was dealer for Hall-Scott engines, manufactured in Berkeley. Seattle took delivery of Hall-Scott-powered Kenworths in 1942 and after the war.

Mack apparatus during this decade were based on the "E" (introduced in 1936 and running through 1951) and the "L" series (introduced in 1940 and extending through 1957). Mack outfitted its own chassis as well as supplying them to other apparatus outfitters. Most major cities and many medium and small departments bought Mack fire apparatus during this period. During this decade Mack was probably the best-known make of apparatus used in cities. Large cities placed orders for scores of Macks.

During the war, Maxim supplied the military with custom apparatus and with fire fighting bodies on commercial chassis. At the war's end, Maxim made an all-out effort to continue as an important presence in the civilian market. One of its efforts was to expand out of the Northeast, where most Maxims were sold. Maxim's aerial ladder, introduced in 1947, was considered to be one of the best in use, and Maxim supplied ladders to other "name" apparatus builders. Streamlined bodies were also offered, with overhead ladder racks and enclosed pump panels.

Late in the decade, Oren began building custom apparatus based on Available chassis. Later, Oren switched to using Corbitt chassis. Two large orders Oren received were from Dallas and Roanoke.

Pirsch received many military orders during the war and was also ready at the war's end to help municipal departments replace their worn-out apparatus. Pirsch aerial ladders were especially popular, with orders coming from cities such as Cambridge, Chicago, Memphis, New York City, Oakland, Philadelphia, and Sacramento.

Seagrave, too, was busy both during and after the war. Its power plant was the venerable V-12 with the designation E-66 (with the two sixes adding up to twelve). Styling changed after the war. In 1949 Seagrave began using rear-mount aerial ladders, which had already been proven in Europe.

After the war, Ward LaFrance offered a new design that featured a three-section grille and full-length doors, extending down to the running boards. The deluxe version came with rear fender skirts. Ward LaFrance's best customer in the immediate postwar era was FDNY, which purchased about eighty pieces of Ward LaFrance equipment. Other orders were received from Baltimore and Philadelphia.

At the war's end, firefighters' salaries began increasing and their hours of labor decreased. The number of on-duty firefighters assigned to each piece of apparatus also decreased. Some fire fighting equipment was re-engineered so that it could be operated with less manpower. In many urban areas, growth was into the suburbs. Fire stations were relocated and had to cover areas with wider geographic dimensions. Radio equipment came into more common use and improved control over apparatus that was away from its station. By 1945 Boston had equipped thirty units, including its three fireboats, with FM two-way radios.[6] In 1948, Rockford, Illinois, announced that all fourteen pieces of its apparatus were equipped with two-way radios.[7]

Salvage corps were being incorporated into municipal departments. Some still existed and continued to buy equipment. Albany bought a 1948 Brockway commercial chassis, which a local body builder outfitted. Baltimore bought a White in 1942, and another in 1943. In the late 1940s, the Boston corps bought several new Fords, as did the corps in Chicago. The New York Fire Patrol switched to Fords, and began enclosing bodies. In 1947 the Worcester salvage corps bought a Buffalo salvage wagon with a four-door cab. Los Angeles purchased three Macks in 1948 to serve as salvage wagons. They each carried fifty 12 x 18 foot waterproof covers, water vacuums, generators, lights, smoke ejectors, sawdust, squeegees, and mops.

By mid-century, modern fire apparatus had evolved. The only two major changes still to come in the truck would be the use of automatic transmissions and of diesel engines. American-LaFrance was the best-known custom apparatus builder, and its cab-forward designs would be copied by nearly all its competitors. Pirsch was the most highly regarded builder of aerials, but in the next half-century other types of elevating devices were to take the place of many aerial trucks. A third change that would take place is a reduction in the size of crew that will ride on each truck. This would mean redesigned equipment that requires less manpower to operate. Lastly, bodies would be designed so that fire crews sat in protective seating, rather than hanging on to the side or rear of the speeding apparatus.

In broad terms, the first half-century included a movement away from horses and steam. Most of the developments of apparatus that are taken for granted today can be traced back to the first half-century. In a subsequent volume, we shall continue our discussion of apparatus, covering the period from 1950 until the present day.

---

[6] *The American City* (January 1945), p. 11.

[7] *The American City* (October 1948), p. 17.

Philadelphia purchased two 1941 Autocars with pipe line pressure wagon bodies, and they were assigned to run as pipe line units 1 and 4. One of these units was later equipped with a large, hydraulically-operated Stang turret gun (a giant deluge unit). That is how it is shown here. It was renumbered as Special Unit 99. (Photo courtesy Dick Adelman)

A 1941 Autocar/U.S. Fire Apparatus 1000 gpm triple combination pumper in service as Engine 9 in Philadelphia. The pumper is open seat. The booster tank is mounted above the pump. The booster hose is carried in a basket tank. (Photo courtesy Charles E. Beckwith)

The U. S. Fire Apparatus Company of Wilmington, Delaware, used a circa-1941 Autocar chassis to finish this sharp-looking 750 gpm pumper for Conshohocken, Pennsylvania. (Photo courtesy Dick Adelman)

Philadelphia purchased thirteen 1941 Autocar 1000 gpm pumpers from the Oren-Roanoke Corporation of Vinton, Virginia. This is Engine 45. Note the circular booster hose basket above the booster tank. (Photo courtesy Wayne Sorensen)

A circa-1941 Central of St. Louis hose wagon. It was in service as Hose Wagon 12 in St. Louis, Missouri. It has a large mounted turret. The rig is based on a GMC chassis. (Photo courtesy Robert Pauly)

Albany, New York, used a 1941 Chevrolet tractor to replace an earlier tractor in front of an American-LaFrance aerial. It ran as Truck 6. (Photo courtesy Wayne Sorensen Collection)

A 1941 GMC that was used as a wrecker by the Boston Fire Department. (Photo courtesy Wayne Sorensen Collection)

Detroit, Michigan, took delivery of this 1941 GMC/General of Detroit city service truck. Note four-door cab. The rig had a chemical tank. (Photo courtesy Dick Adelman)

Baltimore's 1888 Vintage eighty-five-foot Hayes aerial equipped with a Dahill compressed air hoist was described as a "Rube Goldberg"-like concoction. It was coupled with a 1941 Mack "L" Series, Type 19 tractor T-11. Some Hayes aerials were in service eighty-five years. (Photo courtesy John J. Robretch)

Deal, New Jersey, purchased this extra long 1941 Mack "E" Series 500 gpm quad. Note length of cab, with pump in the middle. (Photo courtesy Dick Adelman)

This is a 1941 Mack Type 45 tank wagon placed in service by the City of Los Angeles. It has a three-man cab-over engine, a 150 gpm rotary-gear pump, and a 600-gallon water tank. This rig was part of a two-piece engine company. (Photo courtesy George Bass)

In 1941 the Baltimore Fire Department shops rebuilt a 1917 Mack AC chassis, and added a new Mack front end. The ladder body was originally on a horse-drawn Holloway city service truck. (Photo courtesy John J. Robrecht)

Boston's Engine 36 ran with this 1941 Mack Cardox Wagon. One of the hoses shown was used to apply Cardox; the other hose was connected to a conventional booster system. Note radio antenna. (Photo courtesy Charles E. Beckwith)

In 1941, St. Louis purchased this 1000 gpm Pirsch pumper with an open cab. The siren is mounted next to the cowl. The number of the Engine Company has yet to be painted. (Photo courtesy Pirsch and Dick Adelman)

Miami's Engine 13 was this 1941 Pirsch with an open cab and a 1000 gpm pump. (Photo courtesy Wayne Sorensen Collection)

Parked here is a 1941 Pirsch 1000 gpm pumper used in Memphis. At the time of the photo, Memphis specified that its pumpers be equipped with an extra-long, hard-suction hose connected to a swivel elbow for quick hookups to the water supply. (Photo courtesy Dick Adelman)

The Naval Ammunition Depot at Hawthorne, Nevada, used this 1941 Pirsch 500 gpm pumper that ran on rail tracks. (Photo courtesy Dick Adelman)

Greenville, North Carolina, used this 1941 Pirsch quint. The ladder was sixty feet long, had two sections, was raised manually, and was referred to as a Pirsch "junior" aerial. (Photo courtesy Dick Adelman)

Sacramento bought this Pirsch aerial in 1941. It was a model 77, 100-foot aerial and is shown serving as Truck 10. Currently it is owned by the Sacramento Fire Buff Club. (Photo courtesy Wayne Sorensen)

During World War II some U.S.-built apparatus was given to allied governments under "lend-lease" programs to augment their civilian departments. This 1942 American-LaFrance 100-foot aerial was one of five shipped to Australia. This one was photographed in Brisbane in 1943. Note raised windshield.

This circa-1941 Seagrave Model 80, 750 gpm pumper is hard at work with its hood up at the Naval Operation Base at Norfolk, Virginia. The pumper ran as a hose wagon with Engine 1. (Photo courtesy Dick Adelman)

Philadelphia's Engine 19 was one of fifteen 1941 Ward LaFrance 1000 gpm pumpers the city purchased. On the cowl, note the Roto Rays warning lights. (Photo courtesy John J. Robrecht and Dick Adelman)

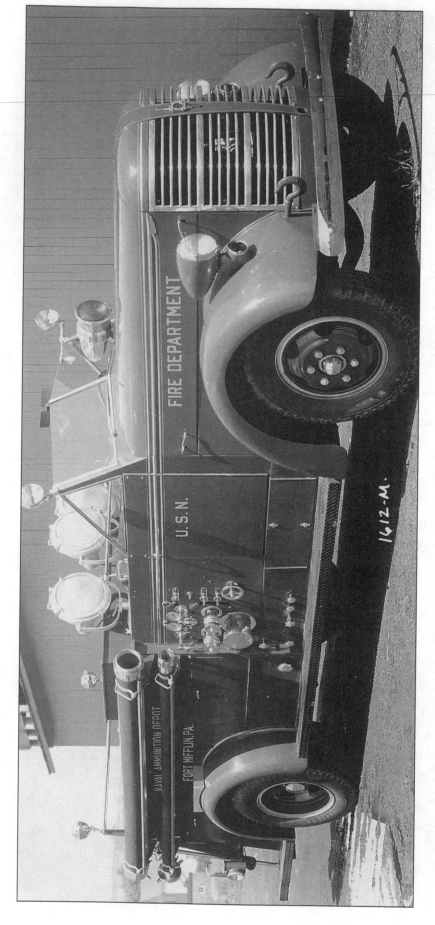

The U.S. Navy Ammunition Depot at Fort Mifflin, Pennsylvania, used this 1942 American-LaFrance 500 Series 750 gpm pumper. (Photo courtesy American-LaFrance)

The United States Army received this 1942, 500 Series American-LaFrance cab model 500 gpm pumper with a chrome bumper. (Photo courtesy American-LaFrance)

This is one of two 1942 American-LaFrance Series 500 tractor-drawn, 100-foot metal aerials used in Chicago. At front is a three-man enclosed cab. In 1953 this rig was reengined with a Cummins diesel. (Photo courtesy Wayne Sorensen Collection)

Harrison, New Jersey, bought this Ahrens-Fox Model HT, 1000 gpm piston pumper in 1942. Sheet metal work reflects a streamlining attempt, compared with earlier models. (Photo courtesy Ernest N. Day)

In 1946 one of San Francisco's wartime auxiliary engines was converted into a coffee van. It was quartered with Engine 4 and would respond to third alarms. This photo, with San Francisco's Bay Bridge in the background, was taken at the 1991 National Fire Buff Convention. (Photo courtesy Wayne Sorensen)

Trenton, New Jersey, built this light truck on a 1942 Chevrolet chassis. No chrome is visible, meaning that the truck was built during World War II. (Photo courtesy John J. Robrecht)

FABCO used a 1942 Dodge chassis to build this 500 gpm pumper with a 200-gallon water tank for the U.S. Army. Wartime apparatus was painted non-lustrous olive drab. (Photo courtesy FABCO)

This is one of two 1942 Dodge/John Bean Fog Firefighter high pressure hose wagons built for San Jose, California. They were equipped with water tanks, high-pressure fog pumps, and two high-pressure hose reels. (Photo courtesy John Bean)

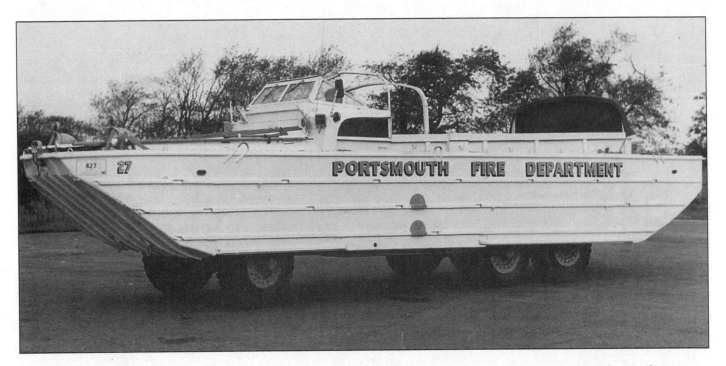

After World War II, surplus military vehicles were available for civilian uses. A few cities purchased ex-military amphibious vehicles to use for rescue work and as small fireboats. This ex-Coast Guard GMC "DUKW" was used in Portsmouth, Rhode Island. (Photo courtesy Dick Adelman)

In 1942 The Hanley Engineering Service of Prospect, Ohio, provided two custom 750 gpm, triple combination pumpers to Marion, Ohio. They were designed by Keenan Hanley and powered by a Marmon V16 engine on a GMC chassis. These pumpers resembled the Ahrens-Fox postwar centrifugal pumpers. They were painted blue and gray. This photo was taken at Harrah's Automobile Collection Warehouse, Sparks, Nevada. (Photo courtesy Wayne Sorensen)

Seven 1942 Mack enclosed cab tractors were placed in service in Chicago. This tractor is attached to a 1927 Chicago Fire Department-built, eighty-five-foot aerial as Hook & Ladder 26. Note life net. (Photo courtesy Dick Adelman)

The New York Port of Embarkation used this 1942 Mack Type 75, 750 gpm pumper.

Seen here is a wartime rig with no chrome. This 1942 E Series Mack, Type 505, 500 gpm pumper was used for plant protection by the Martin Aircraft Company in Omaha. Even the Mack bulldog hood ornament is not wearing its usual chrome coat. (Photo courtesy Dick Adelman)

Huntsville, Alabama, used this circa-1942 Mack Type 72, L Model 750 gpm pumper. It carried only a pump and hose, with no booster equipment, so it could be called a double combination. (Photo courtesy Dick Adelman)

On August 8, 1968, fire broke out in an abandoned natural gas holder in Memphis, Tennessee. A circa-1942 Pirsch pumper is supplying water to a newer Pirsch aerial. There are two large streams coming from the aerial, and at far right, a water tower is throwing water. (Photo courtesy Dick Adelman)

Peter Pirsch & Sons Company built this 1942 sedan cab 1250 gpm pumper for Memphis's Engine 32. This pumper has an extra-long hard-suction hose connected to a swivel elbow for a quick hookup to the water supply. (Photo courtesy Dick Adelman)

Shown here is a 1942 Pirsch Model 20, open-seat, 750 gpm combination pump and hose car that ran as Engine 1 at the Navy Supply Depot, Oakland, California. (Photo courtesy Pirsch)

Two circa-1942 Pirsch pumpers in Memphis working off of a dual hydrant—two steamer connections on a ten-inch main. The first engine inputs a gate valve on one opening so that the second pumper can connect without stopping the water supply. (Photo courtesy Dick Adelman)

Pirsch delivered this quad to Memphis, Tennessee, in 1942. This truck was converted to the Multi-Master, a heavy stream rig that went into service in 1956. The Multi-Master is equipped with ten hose inlets in the rear and twelve discharge gates along the sides. A large hydraulically-operated turret is mounted on top. (Photo courtesy Dick Adelman)

This 1942 Pirsch four-door cab, 1250 gpm pumper served as Engine 32 in Memphis. The suction hose is carried squirrel-tail style around the front of the pumper. (Photo courtesy Dick Adelman)

At the war's end, many military apparatus became available for municipal use. Here is one example, an ex-military Sterling that Pirsch had outfitted with a 750 gpm pump and fire fighting body. (Photo courtesy Dick Adelman)

Newport, Rhode Island, ran this 1942 Seagrave eighty-five-foot aerial ladder as Truck 2. Note "sweetheart" grille.

Seagrave delivered this eighty-five-foot, tractor-drawn aerial to Boise in 1942. Crew seats were located behind the cab seat. This was Boise's Truck No. 1. (Photo courtesy Wayne Sorensen)

The navy used this 1942 Seagrave 750 gpm pumper.

Between 1943 and 1954, the Sanford Fire Equipment Corporation built ten Model N-75 pumpers for the navy. After the war ended, this ex-navy 750 gpm Sanford served Hawaii County, Hawaii. (Photo courtesy Dick Adelman)

This 1942 Ward LaFrance quad ran as Philadelphia's Truck 26. It had a 750 gpm Hale pump, and turned out to be the only quad that Philadelphia used.

This heavy duty wrecker was received from Walter in 1942 by the city of New York. The wrecker is towing a 1930 FWD tractor with a wood aerial. (Photo courtesy Wayne Sorensen)

Ward LaFrance supplied this 1942 model 83T, 750 gpm pumper to Boston, where it ran as Engine 37. It had a Waterous pump. (Photo courtesy F. J. Bertpand)

This 1943 American-LaFrance Model JOX eighty-five-foot service aerial was in service at the U.S. Navy Torpedo Station at Newport, Rhode Island. (Photo courtesy Wayne Sorensen)

Philadelphia's Bureau of Fire used the WW II surplus 1943 Diamond-T with a Holmes twin-boom body as its Emergency Crew 10. Each boom could lift five tons. (Photo courtesy Charles E. Beckwith)

An early 1940s Federal outfitted by General of Detroit and used at the Naval Station at Gulfport, Mississippi. The pump was rated at 750 gpm. The gumball machine warning light was probably added later.

During World War II, the Heil Company, which outfitted petroleum tank trucks, received a large order for fire fighting apparatus to protect military bases and plants. This photo was taken and then labeled for use in a military instruction manual. This truck carries U. S. Navy markings. (Photo courtesy The Heil Co.)

The navy used this early '40s International with an American-LaFrance chemical body as an airfield crash truck. Both International and American-LaFrance emblems are to the rear of the louvres. (Photo courtesy Fred Crismon)

A 1943 "L" Series Mack, war-model (no chrome) tractor attached to a refurbished American-LaFrance aerial in service as Ladder 6 in Bridgeport, Connecticut. (Photo courtesy Dick Adelman)

Some apparatus for the U.S. Navy was built on the West Coast. FABCO used this Mack E chassis to build a small pumper with a Byron-Jackson two-stage 125 gpm centrifugal pump with a 400-gallon tank. (Photo courtesy FABCO)

A fireboat was needed at a supply-unloading point in Guadalcanal in 1944, so an army pumper was carried aboard a small landing craft. (Photo courtesy National Archives)

Baltimore, Maryland's 1944 American-LaFrance Valiant, Series 600, 1250 gpm pumper was in active service until 1961. Then it was kept in reserve as Second Line Engine No. 7. Note the catch-all "Baltimore basket" over the hose bed. (Photo courtesy Dick Adelman)

An enclosed early 1940s Buffalo 750 gpm quad used by the U.S. Navy. (Photo courtesy Buffalo Fire Appliance Company)

Richmond, Virginia, used a 1944 Mack S Series Type 19 tractor to pull a 1919 American-LaFrance eighty-five-foot aerial ladder. (Photo courtesy Dick Adelman)

General of Detroit used a 1945 Available chassis to build this quad for St. Paul. It carried a 200-gallon water tank and a Waterous pump. (Photo courtesy Walt Schryver)

The revolutionary American-LaFrance 700 Series was announced late in 1945. In August, 1947, Washington, D.C. took delivery of this pumper. The 700 Series seated three in front and two in rearward-facing seats on each side of the engine compartment. (Photo courtesy A. Hardy)

Sitka, Alaska used this 1945 500 gpm American-LaFrance Series 500 pumper. The grille is painted mesh. (Photo courtesy American-LaFrance)

A 1946 American-LaFrance Series 600, 1000 gpm pumper in service with Boston, Massachusetts, as Engine 35. The pump and controls are in the cowl. The two stars in the cab window show that two members of this company are serving in the military. (Photo courtesy Charles E. Beckwith)

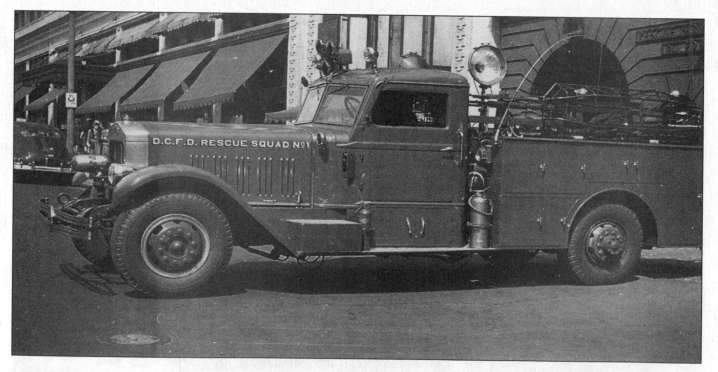

Originally this was a 1929 American-LaFrance booster and hose wagon used in Washington, D.C. In 1931 it was converted to a rescue squad, and in 1946 the fire department's shops enclosed the cab. The headlights shown are sealed-beam. (Photo courtesy Dick Adelman)

The Fresno Fire Department shops built four of these pumpers in 1946. They were equipped with 750 gpm pumps. Peterbilt supplied the radiators and front-end sheet metal. Van Pelt installed the pumps and completed the bodywork. (Photo courtesy Wayne Sorensen)

The Mack E Series was popular in the fire service and kept nearly the same appearance for a decade. This is Grenada, Mississippi's 1946 Mack with a 750 gpm pump and a closed cab. (Photo courtesy Dick Adelman)

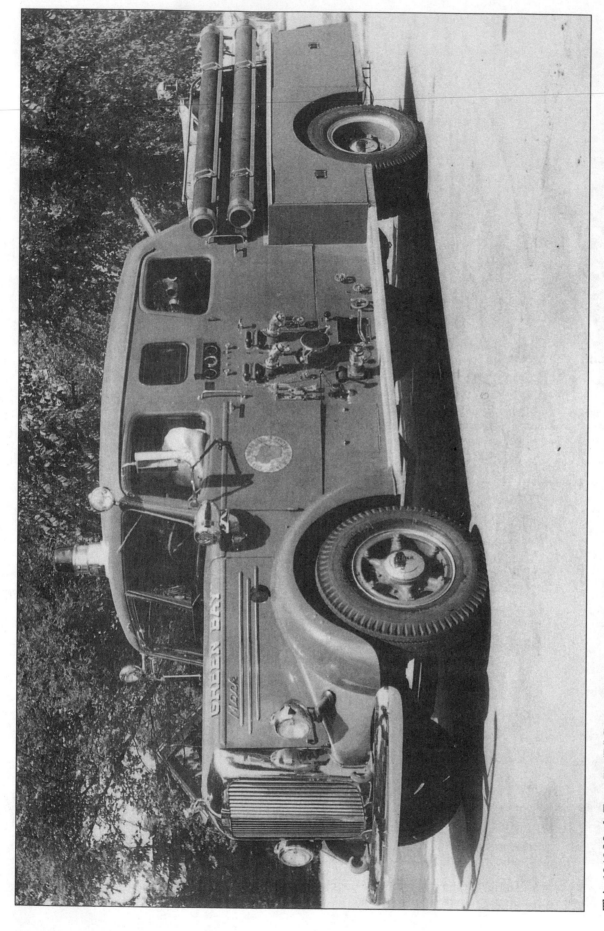

This 1946 Mack Type 75, "L" Series pumper with five-man, four-door sedan cab and 1250 gpm pump was delivered to Green Bay, Wisconsin. The compartments over the rear were added later. (Photo courtesy Dick Adelman)

The 1946 Seagrave 750 gpm triple combination is one of nine identical pumpers purchased by Baltimore. Engine 14 has a fixed turret pipe. The hood is up to cool the engine while pumping. (Photo courtesy Dick Adelman)

A 1947 American-LaFrance Series 700, 750 gpm pumper running as Rescue Squad No. 2 in Washington, D.C. This photo shows the full display of equipment, boots, and gear carried on Squad 2. (Photo courtesy Wayne Sorensen)

One of four 1947 American-LaFrance 700 Series tank wagons delivered to San Francisco. The two hose reels contain 300 feet of one-inch hard rubber hose. They were equipped with a 150 gpm pump and a 400-gallon water tank. The tank wagons were powered by the American-LaFrance V-12, 240 hp motor. Note the crew seating of the 700 Series. (Photo courtesy American-LaFrance)

A 1947 Mack L Model, semi-cab Hose Wagon No. 8 operated by Boston, Massachusetts. It is equipped with a fixed turret pipe, and is powered by the Thermodyne engine. The rear fender has been replaced with a shop fabrication, a common sight on Boston rigs. The front fender is dented, also common to Boston apparatus. (Photo courtesy Dick Adelman)

Oakland, California, purchased two 1947 Pirsch Model 38 city service trucks with water tanks. The power was a 470 Hall-Scott six-cylinder, 275 hp engine. Note the spare tire behind the hose reel. (Photo courtesy Wayne Sorensen)

The shops of the Indianapolis Fire Department rebuilt this 1921 Stutz model B in 1947. Body parts for the rebuild were purchased from the New Stutz Company, and the grille was from a 1937 Diamond-T. The rebuilt unit was powered by a Hercules engine and carried a Northern pump and a small booster tank. Note right-hand steering. (Photo courtesy Dan G. Martin)

One of twenty 1948 American-LaFrance Series 700, 750 gpm pumpers placed in service in New York City. This was Engine 1. Notice the inlets for the deck pipe and the handwheel controlling the turret inlet valve located on the pump panel. (Photo courtesy Frank J. Fenning)

Fire apparatus was often delivered by railroad. Here is a late 1940s American-LaFrance pumper about to be driven off a flatcar after being delivered to Fort Atkinson, Wisconsin. (Photo courtesy Hoard Museum, Fort Atkinson)

Here is Boise's 1948 Ahrens-Fox Model H-C, 1000 gpm pumper used for Engine 5. This pumper has a centrifugal pump, a half-cab, and storage compartments in the rear fenders. (Photo courtesy Wayne Sorensen)

This was one of four 1948 Ahrens-Fox 1000 gpm pumpers ordered by New Orleans. It had a three-man cab and was powered by a Hercules motor. Note Roto Rays lights on top of the pump. (Photo courtesy Dick Adelman)

In 1948, Toledo, Ohio, placed the last order for an Ahrens-Fox service ladder truck. This was a Model 4 ED in service as Ladder 18. (Photo courtesy Wayne Sorensen Collection)

This is one of seven Ahrens-Fox Model JC Spec. 750 gpm pumpers purchased in 1948 by Dallas. This open-seat pumper is powered by a Waukesha Model 145-GKB high output fire engine developing 240 horsepower. (Photo courtesy Waukesha and Wayne Sorensen)

One of four Ahrens-Fox Model AT 1000 gpm piston pumpers with closed cabs that New Orleans purchased in 1948. Note that the cab is more than halfway back on the chassis; soon the industry would shift to cab-forward designs with one advantage being that the driver could see the road directly in front of the truck. (Photo courtesy Dick Adelman)

Philadelphia's Rescue No. 2, a 1948 Brockway with body by Approved Fire Equipment Company. The floodlights retract into the roof. (Photo courtesy John J. Robretch)

Sommerville, Massachusetts, ran as Engine 2 a 1948 Buffalo four-door 750 gpm pumper with enclosed pump compartments. (Photo courtesy M. Young)

Philadelphia operated this 1948 FWD Airport Crash Truck, which carried a 750 gpm pump with six CO_2 cylinders and a 1000-gallon water tank. (Photo courtesy Dick Adelman)

In 1948 the San Jose Fire Department purchased two GMC chassis that Master Mechanic Darwin Cecil built into hose wagons. This is Hose 3 with a fixed 1908 battery. (Photo courtesy Wayne Sorensen)

The fire department shops in Passaic used a 1948 International KB chassis to build this foam/high pressure unit. Two turrets and a foam hopper are visible. (Photo courtesy Dick Adelman)

Providence, Rhode Island, used this 1948 International Metro as its light truck. Note the electrical outlets to the rear of the cab. (Photo courtesy Dick Adelman)

Los Angeles Heavy Utility No. 14, mounted on a 1948 Kenworth chassis, carrying a compressor and a twin-boom wrecker. Power was a Hall-Scott engine. (Photo courtesy Wayne Sorensen)

Engine 42 of Boston, Massachusetts, pumping at a working fire with two charged lines. This 1948 Mack "L" Model has a half-cab, 750 gpm pump. Note the plated radiator shell and the original Mack striping. (Photo courtesy Charles E. Beckwith)

In 1948 Mack supplied Los Angeles with twelve identical Mack Type 95, 1250 gpm pumpers. The pumpers came with half-cabs. Shown is a reserve engine with a fire department shop fabricated cab. (Photo courtesy Paul Darrell)

Maxim apparatus were not common on the West Coast; however, Oakland, California, purchased two Maxim pumpers in 1948. Shown here is Engine 2's 1250 gpm pumper, which had a 200-gallon water tank. It was powered by a Hercules six-cylinder, 238 hp engine. Pump panel is enclosed. (Photo courtesy Wayne Sorensen)

Coast Fire Apparatus of Concord, California, outfitted a 1948 Peterbilt chassis for use in Oakland. The pump was rated at 1250 gpm and there was a 250-gallon booster tank. A Hall-Scott 275 hp engine powered the rig. (Photo courtesy Wayne Sorensen)

This circa-1948 Ward LaFrance was used in Boston as Engine 9. It carried a portable turret pipe, and had booster equipment. (Photo courtesy Charles E. Beckwith)

One of thirty-two 1949 Autocar-U.S. Fire Apparatus 750 gpm triple combinations delivered to Philadelphia. These pumpers had half-cabs and booster reels. (Photo courtesy John J. Robrecht)

A 1949 Chevrolet two-door sedan used to pull an iron lung (for polio victims) in Jersey City.

This is one of eight 1949 Autocar Squad Trucks delivered to Chicago, Illinois. The squads were equipped with a mounted turret and an Aurora Borealis warning light by Mars. Note Stokes rescue basket on side. (Photo courtesy Dick Adelman)

A 1949 FWD pulls an eighty-five-foot wooden aerial in Chicago. The unit ran as Truck 13. Chicago purchased twelve of these trucks. (Photo courtesy Dick Adelman)

This is a 1949 FWD hose wagon in service in Boston, as Engine 21's hose wagon. At this point in time Boston ran two-piece engine companies. The wagon has a half-cab and two mounted turrets. (Photo courtesy Charles C. Beckwith)

With its hood up, Newark, New Jersey's Engine 20 is hard at work. The pumper is a 1949 FWD Model F-100 with a 1000 gpm pump and a 150-gallon booster tank. We see a hard suction hose feeding from the hydrant into the truck's rear inlet. Note hose clamp just this side of inlet. (Photo courtesy Dick Adelman)

Biloxi used this 1949 FWD with its jutting grille and all-wheel drive. This is Engine 4. The pump was rated at 750 gpm. (Photo courtesy Dick Adelman)

In 1949 General-Pacific Corporation assembled this truck using a Kenworth chassis, a 1000 gpm Hale pump, and a Coast body. Power was provided by a Hall-Scott engine. The water tank carried 500 gallons. This truck ran as Engine 260 for the Los Angeles County Fire Department, and was stationed at Universal City. (Photo courtesy Wayne Sorensen)

Boise, Idaho, ran this 1949 International, which had a 750 gpm pump. The body was built by Kinney, of Sacramento. The booster tank carried 150 gallons. (Photo courtesy Wayne Sorensen)

Boston used this circa-1949 Maxim, which had a sixty-five-foot metal aerial, as Ladder 21. A large equipment compartment with two small doors is on the running board. (Photo courtesy Charles E. Beckwith)

Boston's Engine 25 was this circa-1949 Maxim with a 1000 gpm pump. Note the double front bumper. (Photo courtesy Charles E. Beckwith)

Dual-cowl phaeton autos are rare; dual-cowl fire apparatus are even rarer. This 1949 Mack Type 21 "dual-cowl" four-door cab—two windshield—manifold unit was operated by the City of Los Angeles Fire Department. The manifold wagon has a fire boat turret nozzle. It ran with a 1938 American-LaFrance Duplex pumper. (Photo courtesy Glen Alton)

One of eight Type 95 Mack high-pressure hose wagons delivered to the City of Los Angeles from 1948 to 1950. This 1949 wagon had a Morse 1100 gpm turret. It ran as part of a two-piece unit with a Mack 1250 gpm pumper. The wagon had two Byron-Jackson two-stage centrifugal pumps, each rated at 150 gpm. The wagon also had a 400-gallon booster tank. (Photo courtesy Glen Alton)

This is a 1949 Pirsch with an eighty-five-foot wooden aerial ladder, which ran as Truck 19 in Boston. Note dented fenders and non-original grille. (Photo courtesy Dick Adelman)

This is one of eight 1949 Ward LaFrance 750 gpm pumpers that were delivered to Baltimore. This is Engine 29, which has a turret and a 250-gallon booster tank. (Photo courtesy Ward LaFrance)

A 1950 American-LaFrance 700 Series eighty-five-foot aerial powered by the big American-LaFrance V-12 engine. In service as Truck 2, Newark, New Jersey. The photo shows a good view of bed ladders, pikes, aerial control stand, and tiller seat. (Photo courtesy Dick Adelman)

One of two four-door sedan pumpers built by Ahrens-Fox in 1950. This Model H-C 1000 gpm pumper was operated by the Friendship Fire Company of Royersford, Pennsylvania. (Photo courtesy John J. Robrecht and Dick Adelman)

A 1950 Ford Model F-7 chassis was used by Ward LaFrance to build for Philadelphia a hose wagon with fixed turrets, chemical supplies, and smoke ejector. (Photo courtesy John J. Robrecht)

This circa-1950 FWD pumper purchased by New Orleans for Station No. 18 was equipped with a 1000 gpm pump, a 150-gallon booster tank, and a closed cab. The pumper came with the Waukesha six-cylinder, 240 hp engine. (Photo courtesy FWD)

A 1950 Ford Model F-4 chassis used by Ward LaFrance to build this special Service No. 8 light unit for Philadelphia. (Photo courtesy Dick Adelman)

The fire department shops in Atlantic City built this eighty-five-foot aerial truck using an American-LaFrance hoist and a 1950 Ford tractor. (Photo courtesy Robrecht Negatives)

A 1950 Kenworth enclosed cab with Heiser city service truck body. The longest ladder is a fifty-five-foot metal ground extension. The rig is powered by a Hercules 225 hp engine. It was in service as Ladder 7 in Seattle, Washington, until it was converted into an air bottle truck in 1976. (Photo courtesy Heiser)

Seattle ran a large fleet of Kenworth pumpers. In 1946 six 1250 gpm triple combinations were purchased; in 1949 nine 1500 gpm triple combinations were purchased; and in 1950 one 1500 gpm triple combination was purchased. Shown is a 1950 1250 gpm pumper with Hale pump and 200-gallon booster tank. It was powered by a 296 hp Hall-Scott engine. Some of these engines served until 1987. (Photo courtesy Seattle Fire Department)

A Fire and Rescue unit used by the Chicago Civil Defense agency on a circa-1950 Mack LeRoi Compressor truck. (Photo courtesy Wayne Sorensen)

Engine 33 in Boston was this 1950 Mack "R" Series with a 750 gpm pump and a fixed turret. (Photo courtesy Charles E. Beckwith)

This is a 1950 Mack "A" Series semi-cab hose wagon with fixed turret, booster tank, and enclosed compartments. In service as Boston's Wagon 50. (Photo courtesy Dick Adelman)

Pirsch delivered six 1000 gpm combination pumpers to Chicago in 1950. Engine 44 has an International cab and a Hale pump, and is powered by a Waukesha engine. Note the cut-out in the grille for the Mars warning light. (Photo courtesy Bob Freeman and Dick Adelman)

Selected References

A Legend of Service: The History of the Elizabeth Fire Department. (Elizabeth, NJ: Elizabeth Fire Department, 1992).

Birchfield, Rodger. *Stutz Fire Engine Company, A Pictorial History.* (Indianapolis: the author, 1978).

———. *New Stutz Fire Apparatus Co., Inc.* (Indianapolis: the author, 1981).

Burgess-Wise, David. *Fire Engines & Fire Fighting.* (Norwalk, CT: Longmeadow Press, 1977).

Burks, John. *Working Fire--The San Francisco Fire Department.* (Mill Valley, CA: Squarebooks, 1982).

Calderone, John A. *A Guide to Boston Fire Apparatus.* (Staten Island: Fire Apparatus Journal Publication, 1994).

———. *A Guide to New York City Fire Apparatus* (Staten Island: Fire Apparatus Journal Publication, 1990).

Calderone, John A. and Jack Lerch. *Wheels of the Bravest: A History of FDNY Fire Apparatus, 1865-1982.* (Howard Beach, NY: Fire Apparatus Journal Publications, 1984).

California Fire Service Directory (Sacramento: Eldon C. Nagel, 1994).

Cullom, Keith D. and Scott R. Miller. Southern California Fire Service Directory (Goleta, CA: Perfect Image, 1994).

Decker, Ralph and Clyde Talbert. *100 Years of Fire Fighting in the City of Destiny: Tacoma, Washington.* (Seattle: Grange Printing, 1981).

Ditzel, Paul C. *Fire Engines, Fire Fighters.* (New York: Rutledge Books, 1976).

Douglass, Emmons. *While the Flames Raged.* (Middletown, NY: 1993).

Eckart, Harvey. *Mack Fire Apparatus: A Pictorial History.* (Middletown, NY: The Engine House, 1990).

Fire Apparatus Photo Album of the American-LaFrance 150th Anniversary. (Naperville, IL: The Visiting Fireman, 1982).

Fire Apparatus Photo Album of the Greenfield Village Musters. (Naperville, IL: The Visiting Fireman, 1984).

Fire Apparatus Photo Album of the Valhalla Musters. (Naperville, IL: The Visiting Fireman, 1983).

Freidrich, William and Mark Mitchell. *Chicago Fire Department Engines and Hook & Ladders, 1966-1995.* (Deerfield, IL: Blitz Brothers Publications, 1995).

Goodenough, Simon. *Fire: The Story of the Fire Engine.* (Secaucus, NJ: Chartwell Books, 1978).

Goodman, M. W. *Inventing the American Fire Engine.* (New Albany, Indiana: Fire Buff House Publishers, 1994).

Hagy, Steve. *Howe Fire Apparatus Album.* (Naperville, IL: The Visiting Fireman, 1984).

Halberstadt, Hans. *The American Fire Engine.* (Osceola, WI: Motorbooks International, 1993).

Hart, Arthur A. *Fighting Fires on the Frontier*, (Boise, ID: Boise Fire Department Association, 1976).

Hashagen, Paul and Herb Eysser. *Fire Rescue: The History of FDNY Rescue Co. 1.* (Staten Island: 1989).

Hass, Ed. *Ahrens- Fox, the Rolls Royce of Fire Engines.* (Sunnyvale, CA: the Author, 1982).

King, William T. *History of the American Fire Engine.* (Chicago: Owen Davies, 1960).

Klass, George. *Fire Apparatus: A Pictorial History of the Los Angeles Fire Department.* (Inglewood, CA: Mead, 1974).

Lee, Mathew. *A Pictorial History of Seagrave Fire Apparatus.* (Kalamazoo: the author, 1991).

———. Detroit Fire Department Apparatus History, (Kalamazoo: the author, 1989).

Malecky, John M. *Mack Tilt Cab Fire Apparatus.* (Staten Island: Fire Apparatus Journal Publication, 1988).

Matches, Alex. *It Began with a Ronald.* (Vancouver, BC: the author, 1974).

McCall, Walter. *American Fire Engines Since 1900.* (Glen Ellyn, IL: Crestline, 1976).

McNeish, Robert H. *The Automobile Fire Apparatus Operator.* (Los Angeles: The Times-Mirror Press, 1926).

Nailen, Richard L. *Guardians of the Garden City, The History of the San Jose Fire Department.* (San Jose: Smith & McKay, 1972).

Salt Lake City Firemen's Relief Association, *A Pictorial History of the Salt Lake City Fire Department, 1871-1976.* (Salt Lake City: Salt Lake City Firemen's Relief Association, 1976).

Seagrave Motor Fire Apparatus Text Book. (Columbus, OH: Seagrave, 1919).

Semanick, Murray. *Fire Engines.* (New York: Crescent, 1992).

Sorensen, Wayne and Donald F. Wood. *Motorized Fire Apparatus of the West 1900-1906.* (Polo, IL: Transportation Trails, 1991).

Sytsma, John F. *Ahrens-Fox Album.* (Medino, OH: the author, 1973).

Sytsma, John F. and Robert Sams. *Ahrens-Fox, A Pictorial Tribute to a Great Name in Fire Apparatus*, (Medino, OH: the Author, 1971).

Weir, Dick. Iron Men and Iron Machines (Magnolia, Mass., 1976).

Wood, Donald F. and Wayne Sorensen. *American Volunteer Fire Trucks.* (Iola: Krause Publications, 1993).

Wren, James A. and Genevieve J. *Motor Trucks of America.* (Ann Arbor: The University of Michigan Press, 1979).

Also consulted were copies of company literature and catalogs, and of periodicals including *Fire Apparatus Journal, Engine! Engine!, Fire Service Digest, Fire Journal (Pacific Coast), Fire Engineering,* and *The American City*.

INDEX BY MANUFACTURER

INDEX BY LOCATION